EVERY AGE
EVERY STAGE

TEACHING GOD'S TRUTH
AT HOME AND CHURCH

B&H
PUBLISHING
NASHVILLE, TENNESSEE

EVERY AGE
EVERY STAGE

TEACHING GOD'S TRUTH

AT HOME AND CHURCH

Ken
Hindman

Landry
Holmes

Jana
Magruder

978-1-5359-8819-3

Published by B&H Publishing Group
Nashville, Tennessee

Dewey Decimal Classification: 230.07
Subject Heading: DOCTRINAL THEOLOGY / BIBLE—STUDY
AND TEACHING / CHRISTIANITY

All Scripture quotations are taken from the Christian Standard Bible®,
Copyright 2017 by Holman Bible Publishers. Used by permission.

Levels of Biblical Learning® is a federally registered trademark of
Lifeway Christian Resources of the Southern Baptist Convention.

Design by Jennifer Allison, Studio Nth. Illustrations by inithings,
larionova Olga 11, and Amanita Silvicora, shutterstock.
Author photo credits: Ken Hindman by Abbey Dane, Landry Holmes
by Randy Hughes, Jana Magruder by Amanda Mae Steele.

1 2 3 4 5 6 • 25 24 23 22 21

Dedication

From Ken:

Thank you to my wife Kristina for being the perfect
wife, mom, and support to me in ministry. To our boys,
Mack and David, who have walked through every age and
stage of this project. May you both do amazing things for
the Lord and live a Proverbs 3:5-6 life.

From Landry:

To my grandchildren Ian, Mara Ruth, Ezra, Adrian,
and Miriam. May you continue to grow and thrive
"in the training and instruction of the Lord" (Eph. 6:4)
through every age and every stage of your lives.

From Jana:

To the Lifeway Kids Ministry Team—both current
and previous employees—who have spoken into the
Levels of Biblical Learning for many years. Not only have
they helped to create and steward them, they have dedicated
their curriculum development through the lens of
the Levels of Biblical Learning to create trustworthy
content for churches and families everywhere.

Contents

Part 3: How Can My Church Partner with Me?

Appendix

Introduction

There was a time, not so long ago, when my (Jana's) three children were in three different ministries at church: preschool, elementary, and student ministry. I remember my husband and I juggling the drop-off and pick-up procedures for each one and then trying to find each other in time for worship—though we were often late, scrambling to find five seats together in the dark as soon as someone started praying!

While all that might sound somewhat chaotic, we finally got the hang of it! The difficult part of having three kids in three different age groups really showed up in our home discipleship efforts. How could we have family devotions all together when the preschooler couldn't sit still, the elementary kid couldn't focus, and the middle schooler was completely bored and ready to move on to other interests? It was exhausting and discouraging. We wanted to engage our children with Scripture in a meaningful way, but our attempts were geared more to our adult styles of learning, not to how our children were wired to learn at their particular ages and life stages.

When my firstborn was a babe-in-arms, I remember devouring every parenting book I could find, desperately wanting to be the perfect mom. These books were focused on how babies and toddlers develop physically, emotionally, and mentally. I could not wait to witness major physical milestones—eating solid foods and learning to crawl, walk, and run! I was so eager to start teaching her shapes, letters, and numbers; reading and singing to her; and playing puzzles and games with her.

Then her two brothers came along and we were covered up with a baby, toddler, and preschooler! I kept referencing my parenting books over and over again, engaging each child with activities that matched their physical and mental development. And because I wanted them to learn about God from a very early age, I found books and Bible storybooks that helped me teach simple concepts from a very early age. However, as my three kids began growing up, I found myself lost in the mix of starting school, sports, and extracurricular activities, including church.

The parenting books had long been abandoned, and I was treading water! As our children's age gaps began widening, my husband and I found ourselves frustrated when approaching discipleship at home. I now know this is a common scenario for families everywhere. That is why I am so grateful that the Levels of Biblical Learning® were created for moms like me and families like us, who want to disciple our children in the various ages and stages of their lives.

Each spiritual concept area is coupled with a specific level of learning that shows what children can understand about God in an age-appropriate way. I had desperately wanted to help my children through physical and mental milestones, but the missing piece was the spiritual component. What worked in preschool was not working for my second grader. What worked with my second grader was not working for my preteen. The light bulbs came on for my husband and me as we began to engage our children, meeting them where they were in their individual spiritual development, while referencing their cognitive and physical development.

If you are a ministry leader, equipping parents with the Levels of Biblical Learning as outlined in this book could be life-changing for at-home discipleship. And, the coupling of families utilizing this framework of biblical truth while the church is also implementing the tool throughout all the age groups could be transforming for your church and ministry. Imagine a new family visiting your church, checking in their child or teen for the first time. If you could welcome them with a copy of the Levels of Biblical Learning, you could potentially see those same light bulbs that I had begin to illuminate their hearts and minds.

Whether you are a parent or a ministry leader, our families and churches have the opportunity to be powerfully impacted by the use of the Levels of Biblical Learning as a framework of spiritual development at church and home. My prayer is that the light bulbs would shine brightly as you contextualize this incredible discipleship strategy for your family, your church, and your ministry.

Part 1

WHAT ARE THE LEVELS OF BIBLICAL LEARNING, AND WHY SHOULD I CARE?

1

Discipleship and the Levels of Biblical Learning

When I (Landry) was a kid growing up in church, discipleship was a program that met on Sunday nights. In my home, we went to Sunday School and the morning church service on Sunday morning, and on Sunday nights we went to Training Union (later named *Church Training* before being dubbed *Discipleship Training*) and the evening church service. Wednesdays were reserved for church supper, children's choirs, and missions education.

However, the Bible does not restrict discipleship to a time and place. Discipleship is so much more than a program we attend. Rather, discipleship describes how Christians are to live. For the context of this book, *discipleship* is defined as *the process of becoming and being a disciple*. Now, I admit, that's not a very helpful definition without additional explanation of what a disciple is. So, let's start there.

Jesus tells us very clearly to, "Go, therefore, and make disciples of all nations" (Matt. 28:19). But, what is a disciple? The concept of being a disciple did not originate with the New Testament. The prophet Isaiah had disciples (see Isa. 8:16), as did secular teachers and ancient philosophers such as Socrates, Plato, and Aristotle. Basically, a disciple is someone who follows the teachings of another individual, such as a master teacher.

For our purposes, let's define a disciple as someone who trusts Jesus as his or her Savior and Lord and who follows Jesus' teachings. Becoming and being a disciple is a life-long endeavor that commences with receiving God's gift of salvation through Jesus Christ. (See Appendix A: The Gospel, God's Plan for Me.)

Discipleship is not passive. It requires work and usually involves believers speaking into the lives of less mature Christ followers. The primary goal of this book is to equip parents and church teachers to be disciple makers of their children. Whether those children be infants and toddlers, preschoolers, elementary students, middle schoolers, or high school students. Throughout the book, we'll use the terms *kids* and *children* interchangeably to refer to the aforementioned age groups.

The Bible is clear that the primary responsibility of discipling children rests on parents. The most recognized passage is in Deuteronomy where Moses gives these instructions to the Israelites:

> Listen, Israel: The LORD our God, the LORD is one. Love the LORD your God with all your heart, with all your soul, and with all your strength. These words that I am giving you today are to be in your heart. Repeat them to your children. Talk about them when you sit in your house and when you walk along the road, when you lie down and when you get up. Bind them as a sign on your

hand and let them be a symbol on your forehead.
Write them on the doorposts of your house and on
your city gates. (6:4–9)

While God intends for parents to be their children's primary
disciplers, the writer of Psalm 78 builds on the expectations set
forth in Deuteronomy 6 by seeming to indicate that all of God's
covenant people are to play a part in discipling younger gen-
erations. The psalmist writes, "We will not hide them from their
children, but will tell a future generation the praiseworthy acts of
the LORD, his might, and the wondrous works he has performed"
(Ps. 78:4).

The reason for instructing children is simple: "so that they
might put their confidence in God and not forget God's works, but
keep his commands. Then they would not be like their ancestors, a
stubborn and rebellious generation, a generation whose heart was
not loyal and whose spirit was not faithful to God" (Ps. 78:7–8).
For us on this side of the cross, Paul could not be any more clear
about the importance of discipling children than when he reminds
his protégé Timothy, "and you know that from infancy you have
known the sacred Scriptures, which are able to give you wisdom
for salvation through faith in Christ Jesus" (2 Tim. 3:15).

What about kids who have yet to trust Jesus? Can we disciple
them, given our definition of *disciple* assumes a personal relationship with Christ? I believe that we can begin to disciple unbeliev-
ing children by building foundations for discipleship. What are
those foundations? They are biblical truths that ultimately point to
God's redemptive plan through His Son, Christ Jesus.

Those foundations can be found in something called the
Levels of Biblical Learning®, a collection of biblical concepts that

kids learn as they grow from infancy to adulthood.[1] As children grow, they can begin to learn specific biblical concepts, or truths. These concepts are organized by ten major categories: Creation, God, Jesus, Holy Spirit, People, Bible, Family, Community and World, Church, and Salvation.

Each of the ten concept areas includes age-specific biblical concepts that can be learned progressively. We will discover the sequential nature of the Levels of Biblical Learning in Part 2: "How Can I Teach Biblical Truths to My Family at Home?" Before we do, however, let's take a high-level view of how kids learn biblical truth.

Children first learn biblical concepts at various life stages as they hear parents and church teachers tell them Bible stories and talk about Bible truths.[2] Paul reminds us: "How, then, can they call on him they have not believed in? And how can they believe without hearing about him? . . . So faith comes from what is heard, and what is heard comes through the message about Christ" (Rom. 10:14, 17).

Hearing biblical truth that adults tell kids is only the beginning. The next step is for children to know what the biblical concepts mean as they understand and comprehend Bible truths. This knowledge is more than memorization, although that is often an important element. Knowing God's Word includes internalizing Bible truths in both the mind and the heart. Apparently, that's what the people in Berea did after hearing Paul and Silas. "They received the word with eagerness and examined the Scriptures daily to see if these things were so. Consequently, many of them believed" (Acts 17:11–12).

We can tell kids Bible truth, and we can help them understand it. But, is that all we can do? The Bible teaches that obedience is necessary: "But be doers of the word and not hearers only, deceiving yourselves" (James 1:22). Kids who are growing spiritually begin to apply Bible truths to their everyday lives. However, children and teens may not apply Bible truth consistently, just as adults do not always obey God's Word. Parents and teachers will want to continually encourage kids to obey God's teachings.

We desire that our preschoolers, elementary kids, middle schoolers, and high school students learn about Jesus, know Jesus personally, and glorify God as they obey His Word. While we are not responsible for the choices our children make, when we teach them biblical concepts, God can use us to lay foundations for salvation and discipleship.

But, what are those biblical concepts our kids need to learn? As stated previously, they are found in the Levels of Biblical Learning. Think about this idea in the context of building a house. The Levels of Biblical Learning are the blueprints for building the house. Hearing, knowing, and obeying God's Word are the foundation of the house. Preschoolers, elementary kids, preteens, and teenagers are the house that God is building. As parents and church teachers, we follow the plans and lay the foundation. Throughout the process, we trust God to call our children to a personal and eternal relationship with Him through His Son Jesus.

2

Nothing Less than the Bible

As parents, we love getting our children involved with extra-curricular activities. We immerse our kids in lessons and practices, encouraging them to set personal goals and to achieve their best, on a playing field or in a swimming pool, in a concert hall, or in the classroom. Our kids' abilities and their talents are important, but our kids' spiritual lives are even more vital to their development.

In the book *Nothing Less*,[1] I (Jana) wrote that statistics suggest parents do believe they should be the principal instigators of their kids' spiritual development. In fact, 83 percent of parents believe they should be the go-to household authority for questions of matters of spiritual development, but most of these same respondents don't utilize their authority role as proactively as they should. Only 35 percent of parents acknowledge that religious faith is one of the most important influences on parenting, which leaves 48 percent of parents who purport to understand the importance of spiritual development but don't personally act on this need.[2]

More than likely, a majority of Christian parents are simply following the model of how they were discipled. Parents take on the mantle of their children's spiritual development and take their kids to church or other religious activities. However, is making sure our kids are involved in church the most effective way to instill real, lasting, and earnest Christian values in our children's lives?

The reality is that parents are outsourcing more of their children's spiritual development than they may recognize, even if attempted with good intentions. We purport that parents' involvement in their kids' spiritual lives must be personal and personable. This book is intended to help parents and churches develop a partnership in discipling kids, rather than a transactional approach where church leaders and teachers are contractors and parents are the clients.

In 2016, Lifeway Research conducted the Nothing Less study to determine indicators of spiritual health in young adults. While we discovered fifteen influencers of spiritual health, the one characteristic with the largest spiritual impact is Bible reading. Surprised? We were. Of all the activities that children engage in, regular Bible reading while growing up was the number one indicator of spiritual health of young adults.[3]

This fact is why the Levels of Biblical Learning is such an important tool for parents and churches desiring to partner together. We want to ensure our kids are exposed to Bible truths throughout their lives while growing up. The statements listed in the Levels of Biblical Learning provide us with a blueprint for doing just that. Part 2 of this book provides practical ways to encourage our preschoolers, elementary students, preteens, and teenagers to engage in regular Bible reading in a systematic way that helps them learn and apply Bible truths. Fundamental to helping our kids develop a desire to spend time in God's Word is teaching them how to memorize Scripture and providing them with their own copy of the Bible.

The psalmist writes, "I have treasured your word in my heart so that I may not sin against you" (Ps. 119:11). The implication is clear: memorization is one of the keys to hiding God's Word in our hearts so that God can use it to change us and grow us in His will. However, memorizing Bible verses is more than just recalling words. To truly know God's Word, we must allow the Holy Spirit to write God's Word on our hearts. The psalmist goes on to say, "I will meditate on your precepts and think about your ways. I will delight in your statutes; I will not forget your word" (Ps. 119:15–16).

Since we know that God uses Scripture to impact kids' lives, plan more than a one-time use of a Bible verse.[4] As a result, the divinely inspired words may impact kids for a lifetime. Also, we know that children absorb new material gradually. On an average, the younger the child, the fewer verses he or she can be expected to learn and relate to life. In a similar vein, children and teens differ in their abilities. Some kids can memorize words and grasp meanings more quickly than their peers. Therefore, the more often a Bible verse is used and recalled, the better a child or teenager will remember and apply it. Finally, while rote memory is a time-honored tradition, today's kids are more interested in learning when methods are varied and engaging. Their learning is enhanced when they are involved in activities designed to teach the words and meaning of Bible verses in age-appropriate ways.

Congruous to encouraging kids to memorize Scripture is ensuring they have a copy of the Bible that fits their particular life stage. I (Landry) still have the first full-text Bible that I could call my own. While my engraved name on the leather cover has faded to near obscurity, I still treasure this gift from my parents. On the presentation page, my dad inscribed that I received the Bible on the occasion of my "request and love for this Book." Since that time, publishers have made great strides in creating Bibles that assist preschoolers, elementary kids, preteens, and teenagers in personal Bible reading and study. In fact, the choosing of the right Bible for our children can be overwhelming.

A Bible is one of the most valuable gifts you can give your child. The value of the Bible you choose is not dependent upon whether or not it is expensive. The Bible's value lies in the fact that it is God's Word. Choose a Bible that will last for several years. As your child grows, consider providing a Bible designed for his or her age group.

For preschoolers and younger children, the Bible should be large enough for the child to hold easily, but not too large or heavy to carry. Consider a tote to help him carry his Bible.

Whether your child is a preschooler, a teenager, or somewhere in between, give him or her a complete Bible. Kids need to know that both Testaments are included in the Bible and are equally important. Bible storybooks are great to use at home as a companion to the full-text Bible. Also, consider a Bible that contains a Table of Contents to assist school-age children in locating hard-to-find books and verses in the Bible.

Realistic illustrations help preschoolers and young children realize that people and stories in the Bible are real and true. In addition, an accurate, reliable, and readable translation of the biblical text rather than a paraphrase will help kids memorize and recall Bible verses. Bibles with study helps can aid elementary kids in learning about the customs and lifestyles of the people in the

Bible. Preteens and teenagers may benefit from a study Bible with commentary notes or even an apologetics study Bible.

I will never forget going to the Christian bookstore with my dad in 1971 to choose my first Bible. The fact that I was able to quickly find it on my bookshelf as I write these words is a testament to the fact that I still cherish my first copy of God's Word. No matter the age of your child, he or she will have a greater sense of ownership if allowed to help choose his or her own Bible. And, that is just the beginning of a life-long lesson that nothing less than the Bible is essential to our spiritual growth.

3

Discipleship Toolbox

Now that we have defined discipleship and have established the fact that nothing less than Bible reading is the primary indicator of discipleship, the logical next step is to determine how to disciple babies, preschoolers, elementary kids, preteens, and teenagers. In order to disciple kids at home and church, we need appropriate tools.

When I (Landry) was a preteen, my dad decided the time had come for me to start building my own collection of tools so he invested in a durable toolbox. At first my toolbox seemed huge because of all the empty air it contained. However, over the years as I have been gifted tools and as I have made my own purchases, my toolbox has become a treasure trove almost too heavy to carry. My dad also purchased toolboxes and starter tools for my two sons when they were kids. Almost every Christmas I carry on the tradition by gifting my now adult sons with tools.

In order to teach God's truth to children and teens, we need tools. The first and most important tool is the Bible. We cannot disciple our kids without the Bible. To attempt to do so would be akin to hammering a nail with a screwdriver. It can be done, but the results are a bent nail and possibly a bruised thumb. Consider the Levels of Biblical Learning and this book as additional tools to place in your toolbox. As your own children and the kids at church grow in their understanding of biblical truth, you may add other tools to the toolbox.

Now, it's one thing to possess a tool and it's quite another to know how to properly use the tool. I enjoy watching my young grandchildren play with toy tools. One of the first actions they perform with a plastic hammer is to hold the head of the hammer and bang the handle against an object. For optimal use of this book, let's take some time to explore the best way to use it as a tool so that we're not trying to drive a nail with the handle.

The heart of this book is found in "Part 2: How Can I Teach Biblical Truths to My Family at Home?" Each chapter is dedicated solely to one of the ten biblical concept areas. While it's possible to skip around and only read the chapter on a particular biblical concept and to read just the sections that apply to your own children, we recommend that you first read the chapters completely and in order. This approach will help you understand the overall discipleship plan that this book provides. Then, come back to select chapters and sections as you seek to employ the ideas in your parenting and teaching experiences during the various stages of your child's spiritual journey. You may even choose to use the ideas in Part 2 for your family devotion times.

You'll notice that each chapter in Part 2 begins with a brief introduction of the biblical concept area for your own edification as a parent or teacher. Following that is a three-step discipleship process. The first step is to read the Bible with your child. (Remember what we said about the Nothing Less research?) Digital versions are great for accessibility and mobility; however, I suggest you use a physical Bible. When your children see you using a Bible with ink on paper, they are more apt to associate the words with truth and real events. Also, I have discovered that we can transfer skills we learn by using a physical Bible to the use of a Bible on an electronic device; however, learning Bible skills on a digital Bible is quite limited.

The second step involves thinking about the Bible. The psalmist reminds us that, "happy is the one [whose] delight is in the LORD's instruction, and he meditates on it day and night" (Ps. 1:1–2). Take time for personal reflection on God's Word and ask for Godly wisdom to teach Bible truth to your kids. Also, help your children meditate on what you have read in the Bible. Lead them to join King David in praying, "May the words of my mouth and the meditation of my heart be acceptable to you, LORD, my rock and my Redeemer" (Ps. 19:14).

Step three is the most detailed portion of each of the ten chapters in Part 2. In this section you'll find practical ideas of how to teach your preschoolers, elementary students, preteens, and teenagers the Bible. This part of the chapter is subdivided into the eight age groups that we will define shortly. Within each age group, we list specific biblical concept statements from the Levels of Biblical Learning. These are the particular Bible truths we want to guide each respective age group to discover. Then, we suggest Bible-learning activities for younger preschoolers through middle elementary students.

Beginning with preteens and extending through the teenage years, we recommend using Bible conversation starters to help older kids and students grapple with how God's Word applies to their lives. For high school students, we have provided additional ideas to help them dig deeper in biblical truth. Under the subheadings of *Being*, *Doing*, and *Apologetic*, you'll find specific ways that older students can relate to God, live out their faith, and explain and defend their faith to others. For additional supporting activities and conversation starters, check out the suggestions at lifeway.com/lobl.

Throughout Part 2, you'll see generic age groupings rather than specific age designations. The reason for this is two-fold. First, kids go through life stages at different rates. For example, a two-year-old in one family may be completely potty trained, while her playmate may not go to the restroom on his own consistently until he's almost four. As you read the Levels of Biblical Learning truths, you may discover that your child relates to more than one age group's biblical concept statements. A second reason we use generic classifications of ages is because churches vary in how they group kids. An older child may be part of the preteen ministry of her church, and when she visits her friend's church she may be directed to the middle school or student ministry.

Nonetheless, I often find having a general idea of specific age designations helpful. So, for the purposes of this book we'll define ages in this way:

- Younger Preschool: zero to twenty-four months
- Middle Preschool: two- and three-year-olds
- Older Preschool: four- and five-year-olds
- Younger Elementary Kids: six- and seven-year-olds
- Middle Elementary Kids: eight- and nine-year-olds
- Preteens: ten- and eleven-year-olds
- Middle School: twelve- and thirteen-year-olds
- High School: fourteen-year-olds to eighteen-year-olds

Keep in mind that these age definitions are flexible, so adjust as needed for your family or ministry environment.[1] One of the reasons you may find flexibility necessary is if your child has special needs. In that case, select the age group that most closely fits your child's developmental needs and teach him or her those biblical concepts.

While Part 2 of this book occupies the bulk of the page count, this tool would be incomplete if we neglected to examine how the home and church can come alongside one another to disciple babies through high schoolers. We'll do that in Part 3 by answering the question, "How can my church partner with me?"

Let's acknowledge, though, that home and church partnerships don't always come to fruition. Some of the kids that show up at our churches do not have Christian parents to guide them on their spiritual journey. Other kids may be living with grandparents or foster parents. In every unique family situation, the church will need to make adjustments to help families meet children's discipleship needs, making the suggestions in Part 2 just as applicable to the church as to the home. Likewise, some churches may lack the vision or resources to disciple kids of all ages appropriately. If this is the case, then parents and other Christian adults will need to take up the slack.

So are you ready, parent? Are you ready, church leader or teacher? Let's open our toolbox and start discipling our infants, preschoolers, elementary kids, preteens, and teenagers!

Part 2

HOW CAN I TEACH BIBLICAL TRUTHS TO MY FAMILY AT HOME?

4

Teaching My Family about God's Creation

Creation is everywhere! God's creation is easy to locate and find. You look to the sky, you see God's creation. You look to the ground, you see God's creation. You look to the oceans, lakes, rivers, and streams; you see God's creation. Everywhere you go and everywhere you look, you see God's creation. Regardless of the age of your child, you can start the process of discipleship and spiritual growth by teaching him/her about God's amazing creation.

Read the Bible

Open to the first book of the Bible. Genesis was written by a man named Moses and gives a detailed narrative of all of the things that God created for us to enjoy. Read Genesis 1:1–25. In these passages you see the detailed order the Creator used to call all of His creation into being. Read Genesis 1:26–31. What does God say about His creation? Throughout chapter 1, we read that everything God made was good, then in verse 31, the writer says that all of creation was "very good." Paul echoes that truth in the

New Testament when he writes, "For everything created by God is good" (1 Tim. 4:4).

Think about the Bible

God made so many things for us to enjoy, and you have the opportunity to introduce your child to the Creator's most amazing creation. Take a moment to personally reflect on all of the beautiful things God created. What comes to mind? Maybe a beautiful flower, a flowing stream, a full moon in the autumn sky, a bird gracefully flying through the sky, a butterfly, a giraffe, or a tiny kitten? What words can you use to describe the beauty you have just envisioned in ways that children with limited experiences can understand? As you teach your kids about creation, allow God to give you a renewed sense of wonder regarding everything He has made. God's creation is all around us. There are so many amazing truths that you are going to want to share with your child. Be creative. Make learning fun, age-suitable, and interesting.

Teaching Younger Preschoolers about Creation

Use the following statements and activities to teach your younger preschooler about the beautiful world God has made.

Biblical Concept Statements

- God made day, night, plants, sky, sun, moon, stars, animals, water, birds, fish, and people.
- God made people.
- God made food for people and animals.

- God planned for people to care for the things He made.
- God said His creation is good.
- God wants me to thank Him for the things He made.

Bible-Learning Activities

God made day, night, plants, sky, sun, moon, stars, animals, water, birds, fish, and people.

Make a "Creation Box." Place in a box or basket some items related to creation, such as a flower, a piece of fruit, a leaf, a stuffed animal, a baby doll, a star, a picture of a snowflake, a bottle of water, a seashell, etc. As you hold your child, choose an item from the Creation Box and share it with your child. Talk about the fact that God made that item for you to enjoy. If you choose the piece of fruit, say that God made fruit on the third day of creation for us to eat. You may choose to feed your preschooler the fruit and thank God for His creation. Keep the Creation Box for a few days and continue teaching your child about God's creation.

God planned for people to care for the things He made.

Gather a baby doll that can get wet, a towel, small washcloth, and dishpan filled with no more than two inches of water. Guide your preschooler to wash and dry the doll. Mention that God planned for us to care for all the things He has made. Talk about ways we can care for God's creation, including caring for the family pet and planting flowers. Lead your preschooler to thank God for His creation.

Teaching Middle Preschoolers about Creation

Take advantage of your middle preschooler's propensity to enjoy playing outdoors. As you spend time with your child outside, use the following suggestions to teach your preschooler about God's creation.

Biblical Concept Statements

- God created the world in six days and rested on the seventh.
- God made people different from the other things He made.
- God cares for His creation.
- God has people to care for His creation.
- God wants me to like His creation too.
- God wants people to thank Him for the things He made.
- God made people able to love.

Bible-Learning Activities

God made people different from the other things He made.

Gather a baby doll and your child's Bible. Read Genesis 1:26–27 aloud and state, "God made people and God made you. God made you to be a [handsome little boy or beautiful little girl]." Encourage your preschooler to hold and hug the baby doll. Comment that God made people different from all other things. Ask him how we are different from giraffes, elephants, birds, fish, etc. Pray, thanking God that He made us special.

God cares for His creation, and God has people to care for His creation.

Collect a few of the following items: nuts, beans, vegetables, and fruit. Say, "God made food for people to eat, and God made food for animals to eat." Lead your preschooler to name some of the foods that animals and people eat. Point out that some animals eat the same kinds of food that we eat. God cares for everything that He made, and He provides food for His creation. Consider going to a zoo, aquarium, farm, or pet store. Talk about the people who feed the animals and remind your child that God planned for people to take care of His creation.

Teaching Older Preschoolers about Creation

Older preschoolers can start learning about the responsibility God has given them to help take care of His creation. Use the following suggestions to encourage your child to be a good steward of all God has created.

Biblical Concept Statements

- God created the world in six days and rested on the seventh.
- God created people able to make choices.
- God provides for His creation.
- God planned for people to care for the things He made.
- God wants me to enjoy the things He created.
- God wants people to thank and praise Him for His creation.
- God made people able to love Him.

Bible-Learning Activities

God planned for people to care for the things He made.

Most likely, your preschooler is ready and eager to help you care for His creation. Cultivate a flower bed or make a container garden with your child. Allow your child to help you choose flower seeds, vegetable seeds, or seedlings to plant. Demonstrate how to plant and care for the seeds or seedlings. Your preschooler will have fun keeping the seeds and plants watered, so consider purchasing a child-size watering can for her to use. Talk about how God provides sunshine and water and makes the plants grow.

God wants me to enjoy the things He created.

Most kids enjoy playing outside. While your preschooler plays, talk about God's creation and how God wants us to enjoy it. In addition to playing outside, plan a family star-gazing party. All you need is a blanket, snacks and drinks, and a cloudless night. As you lie with your child on the blanket, try counting the stars and point out that God made all the stars in the sky. Also, don't forget to talk about the moon. Thank God for all the good things He made that we can enjoy.

God created people able to make choices, and God made people able to love Him.

Play a choices game with your child. Place a piece of red construction paper on one side of the room and a green sheet of paper on the opposite side. Ask your older preschooler to name some choices he can make. Mention that sometimes we make right choices and occasionally we make wrong choices. Name some right and wrong choices and guide your child to stand by the red paper if it's a wrong choice and the green paper if it's a right choice. Say, "God helps us make good choices and one of those choices is to love God." Your preschooler learns to love when he sees you demonstrate love. As your child observes you being kind, tell him that we help others because we love God.

Teaching Younger Elementary Kids about Creation

Your child may start to hear theories about how the world was created. Use the following biblical concepts and suggested activities to help your child understand that God created the world and everything in it.

Biblical Concept Statements

- God created the world from nothing.
- God created everyone to be like Him and to have a relationship with Him.
- God planned and provided for His creation.
- God planned for people to care for His world.
- God is still at work in His creation.
- God is to be praised for His creation.
- God made people able to love Him and others.

Bible-Learning Activities

God created the world from nothing.

Gather some readily accessible craft supplies such as construction paper, paper plates, chenille stems, or play dough. Guide your child to make something using the supplies. Ask her to tell you about what she made. Avoid potential embarrassment by not asking, "What is it?" Point out that God made the world from nothing. Say, "You used art supplies for your creation, but God started with nothing." Lead your child to worship and serve our very creative God!

God created everyone to be like Him and to have a relationship with Him, and God made people able to love Him and others.

Number six pieces of paper one through six. Place the numbered sheets of paper around the room. Walk with your child to each numbered paper and help him recall what God created on each day of creation. When you arrive at the sixth paper, talk about how God made people different from the animals. Say, "Only people can have a relationship with God and that is why God made us able to love Him and others." Your child will learn to love God and others by watching and listening to you. Tell your child every day that you love him. Read together Jesus' words, "I give you a new command: Love one another. Just as I have loved you, you are also to love one another. By this everyone will know that you are my disciples, if you love one another" (John 13:34–35).

Teaching Middle Elementary Kids about Creation

Middle elementary kids still can be in awe of God's creation. They also are curious about how things work. Use the following concept statements and activity suggestions to explain how everything in creation works exactly as God has planned.

Biblical Concept Statements

- God created people in His image.
- God spoke the world into existence from nothing.
- God's creation follows His plan.
- God wants people to take responsibility for taking care of His creation.
- God is still at work in His creation and cares what happens in it.
- God wants people to praise Him for His creation.
- God made people in His image to have a personal relationship with Him.

Bible-Learning Activities

God is still at work in His creation and cares what happens in it.

Do you ever get the feeling that everything is out of control? Even if it seems that way, we know that God is in complete control. He is all-powerful, sovereign, and good. The Creator is still at work and cares so much about what happens in the world He created. Watch or listen to the weather forecast with your child. Mention that even the most accomplished meteorologist does not forecast the weather with 100 percent accuracy. They are not in control. But God is. Our heavenly Father is in control over the wind blowing, rain falling, thunder clapping, and lightning striking. Ask your child what happens after every thunderstorm. Even after the most devastating storm, the sun eventually shines. I believe that is one way God shows He cares about creation, and God cares about you and your child.

*God made people in His image to have a personal
relationship with Him.*

Provide your child with washable markers and a mirror.
Guide her to draw a picture of her face on the mirror. Ask, "Does
your picture look exactly like you?" Read Genesis 1:26–27 in your
child's Bible. Say, "When God made us in His image, He didn't
create us to look or be exactly like God. However, to be made
in God's image means that we have the unique ability to have
a personal relationship with our Creator. Nothing else in God's
creation can know and glorify God the same way that people
can." To help your child understand how we can have a personal
relationship with God, talk through "Appendix A: The Gospel,
God's Plan for Me."

Teaching Preteens about Creation

Use the following statements and Bible conversation starters
to teach your preteen about God's marvelous creation. Encourage
your child to put down the video game controller and spend time
outside.

Biblical Concept Statements

- Creation can be credited only to God.
- God created people in His image.
- God's world is orderly, following God's purpose.
- God gives people the responsibility to care for His
  creation.
- God is still at work in His creation, cares what hap-
  pens in it, and is working out His plan through it.

- God wants people to praise Him for His creation.
- God restores our relationship with Him when we trust Jesus as Savior and Lord. Our response is worship.

Bible Conversation Starters

Creation can be credited only to God.

Ask your preteen to list his three favorite things that God created and to give the reason why he chose those items. Be willing to wait for his response because a preteen's brain requires time to process the question and answer. Follow your kid's response by asking, "On what day(s) of Creation did God create those three things? Who else other than God could have made your favorite creations?" Point out that only God the Father could have created those items. Say, "God created everything, and all of creation belongs to Him."

God wants people to praise Him for His creation.

Ask your preteen what it means to give God praise. Giving praise to God for His creation is accomplished by telling and giving Him credit through our words that an item in creation is amazing. Remind your preteen that all the praise belongs to God, the Creator of everything. Teach your child to share in her own words through prayer that she is impressed by all that God has made. You may want to give her the option of writing her prayer and placing it in a location where she'll see the prayer often and be reminded to give praise to God.

Teaching Middle Schoolers about Creation

Use the following statements and Bible conversation starters to teach your middle schooler about God's marvelous creation. When your child questions the truth of some of the biblical concept statements, listen without reacting. Acknowledge doubt and don't condemn. Doing so will leave open the door to teach God's truth over time.

Biblical Concept Statements

- God is Creator, and all creation is a result of His work.
- Creation testifies as to the existence of God, and people are without excuse for their disbelief and disobedience.
- God's creation functions in an orderly way and serves His purposes as He continues to work in His creation.
- God has given people responsibility for overseeing His creation, and we should steward it for His purposes.

Bible Conversation Starters

God is Creator, and all creation is a result of His work.

Ask your middle school student the following question: "Who made the _____ [fill in the blank with something God created]?" Continue to ask the same question with different items filling the blank until your middle schooler comments on your asking so many questions. Point out that God is the only One who could have made the items you mentioned. God created everything! All of creation belongs to Him and is a result of His work.

Creation testifies as to the existence of God, and people are without excuse for their disbelief and disobedience.

The biblical truth that all creation points to God and testifies to God's existence may be difficult for your middle schooler to comprehend and defend. Ask your middle schooler how he would respond to a friend or acquaintance who questions what your kid knows about creation and the Creator. Supplement your child's reply by pointing to and memorizing key verses such as Genesis 1:1–2; Romans 1:20; and Hebrews 11:3.

God's creation functions in an orderly way and serves His purposes as He continues to work in His creation.

Share with your middle schooler that God created order to His world. Review what God created on each day of creation. Ask, "Why do you think God created plants on the third day of creation? What needed to exist before God created animals on the sixth day?" Remind your child that God spoke all things into being in an orderly fashion to accomplish His purposes. Continue to discuss how things work in the universe, and point to the evidence of God's continuous and orderly creative work.

Teaching High Schoolers about Creation

At this point in your child's life, his level of understanding related to God's creation most likely is solidified. However, is your high schooler ready to defend his Christian beliefs? Discern your high schooler's knowledge of creation and the Creator as you use the following statements and Bible conversation starters.

Biblical Concept Statements

- God is Creator, and all creation is a result of His work and exists to glorify Him.
- Creation testifies as to the existence of God, and because His power and nature are understood through what He has made, people are without excuse for their disbelief and disobedience.
- God's creation functions in an orderly way and serves His purposes as He exercises sovereign rule over it all.
- People are God's most loved creation and have been given responsibility for overseeing His creation. As we steward it for His purposes, we reflect God's character and authority.

Bible Conversation Starters

Creation testifies as to the existence of God, and because His power and nature are understood through what He has made, people are without excuse for their disbelief and disobedience.

Read Genesis 1:1–2, Romans 1:20, and Hebrews 11:3 with your student, using more than one Bible translation. Ask, "Are there any viable options for how the world came into existence other than what the Bible teaches? Why or why not?" Lead your high schooler to a deeper understanding of how creation itself points to our Creator God.

God's creation functions in an orderly way and serves His purposes as He exercises sovereign rule over it all.

Guide your high schooler to think about the differences between each day's creation. Talk about both the simplicity and complexity of creation. Remind your student that creation serves God's purposes and that God spoke all things into being in an orderly fashion. Ask, "Why was it important for God to create the world sequentially? What evidence points to God's sovereign rule, whether or not people acknowledge that fact?"

Digging Deeper in Biblical Truth

Use the statements below to help your high schooler think deeply about creation and be prepared to defend his beliefs.

Being: God created a universe, which was whole and good, but humanity's sin brought brokenness, pain, and relational separation between God and people. However, those who are part of God's family are new creations in Christ and will dwell with God in the new heaven and earth.

Doing: As those whom God has entrusted with the responsibility of overseeing His creations, we should steward well all the things God gives us in a way that honors Him and points others to Jesus.

Apologetic: God created the world; therefore, it belongs to Him. Upon placing people in the garden, He called us to rule over the world as an expression of His authority. Because we have the responsibility of caring for the world and all its resources, we must steward it well as God would.

5

Teaching My Family about the Bible

Did you know that the Bible is the most reproduced, reprinted, read, and quoted book in history? The Bible is a collection, or canon, of religious texts that are sacred to Christians. The entire text is the inspired Word of God; consists of sixty-six books; and is filled with hymns, prayers, proverbs, letters, poetry, prophecies, laws, history, and an overall telling of God's story. The Bible was inspired by the Almighty God and for centuries has had a profound influence on literature, history, music, entertainment, and pop culture. Some even believe that the Bible has done more to shape culture than any other book ever written. The Bible was the first book printed using movable type and has sold well over five billion copies, making it the all-time best seller.

Read the Bible

Read Isaiah 40:8. What does the prophet Isaiah say is the only thing that will last forever? Now, read John 21:25. Does the Bible contain all there is to know about Jesus? There is so much information in the Bible to share with our kids that if you start today, you will still discover new and exciting truths until the day you breathe your last breath. Finally, read Revelation 22:18–19. What do these two verses indicate about the sacred nature of the Bible?

Think about the Bible

Do you have a Bible in your house? Do you have a copy of the Bible downloaded on your mobile device? Do your kids have a copy of the Bible they call their own? Do you read your Bible on a regular basis? Do you memorize key Bible passages? While I (Ken) can answer each of those questions affirmatively, please know that I am in no way trying to boast or brag. I do want you to know, though, that the Bible is the most important instruction book in my life. I have several in my office, but the one I use most is extremely personal to me. I read it, make notes in it, use it as a study guide, use it as a teaching guide, and use it to teach kids and their families. I dearly love my Bible. I pray that as you read this chapter, you will develop a passion for biblical truth. And that you will have a deep desire to teach your infant, toddler, preschooler, elementary child, preteen, and teenager the Bible so one day they can say with the psalmist, "I have treasured your word in my heart so that I may not sin against you" (Ps. 119:11).

Teaching Younger Preschoolers about the Bible

As a parent, I pray you grasp the excitement of teaching your young child the Bible and all the biblical truth it contains. If you haven't already, consider purchasing a durable Bible for your preschooler. Remember, kids this age drop things, put things in their mouths, and rip pages. Sometimes they might use a crayon, pencil, or marker to draw and color on the pages. Gently redirect your child as you teach him the following biblical concepts.

Biblical Concept Statements

- The Bible is a special book.
- The Bible tells about God.
- People in the Bible told about God.
- The Bible tells about Jesus.
- The Bible helps me know what to do.

Bible-Learning Activities

The Bible is a special book.

From the first time you open the Bible and read any passage to your child, teach her that the Bible is a special book. One way to teach this concept is to model touching, holding, looking at, and reading the Bible. Doing so will help your young preschooler know to treat the Bible with respect, love, tenderness, and care. With your child sitting in your lap, hold the Bible open to 2 Timothy and read or paraphrase 2 Timothy 3:16.

The Bible tells us about God and the Bible tells us about Jesus.

Use sticky notes or strips of various colors of construction paper to mark various Bible verses in your Bible and in your child's Bible. With your preschooler sitting in your lap, say, "We're going to play a Bible game. Point to the red Bible marker." Next, read or paraphrase the verse. As you read each verse, pause and say, "The Bible tells us about God and Jesus." Possible Bible verses to use are

Genesis 1:1; Deuteronomy 6:5; Luke 2:52; and 2 Timothy 3:15. Continue playing as long as your preschooler shows interest.

Teaching Middle Preschoolers about the Bible

This is such a fun age to engage in Bible learning. Your two- or three-year-old will believe everything you say. When you teach your child about the Bible, you'll want to be sure your words are biblically accurate. That doesn't mean you need to tell them every detail. (After all, the Bible does include violence and sex.) Also, there is no need to embellish Bible stories. Therefore, use the following biblical concept statements and Bible activity suggestions as you teach your preschooler biblical truths.

Biblical Concept Statements

- The stories in the Bible are true and really happened.
- The Bible teaches us what God is like.
- People wrote God's words in the Bible.
- The Bible teaches what Jesus did.
- The Bible teaches me right and wrong.

Bible-Learning Activities

The stories in the Bible are true and really happened.

With your preschooler sitting in your lap or nearby, open your Bible to Genesis 1. Read or tell the creation story in your own words. Say, "Everything we read in the Bible really happened." Encourage your child to sing with you this simple song to the tune of "Mary Had a Little Lamb": "The Bible is a special book, special book, special book. The Bible is a special book. It tells of

God's great love." Repeat, substituting phrases such as, "it came from God above," "it tells of God's own Son," and "let's learn and have some fun."

The Bible teaches me right and wrong.

Gather paper, crayons or washable markers, and glue (optional). Your preschooler is learning at a fast pace. She is learning how to obey and follow rules. Help your child draw pictures of ways that kids can be obedient, such as making up the bed, picking up toys, setting the table, and taking care of a pet. As an option, you may choose to print pictures from the Internet or cut pictures out of a magazine and glue them to the paper. Mention, "The Bible says, 'Children, obey your parents in the Lord, because this is right' (Eph. 6:1). You are doing what the Bible says is right when you obey Mommy and Daddy."

Teaching Older Preschoolers about the Bible

For many of us, our earliest Bible story memories are from our older preschool years. Stories such as, "God Made the World," "God Took Care of Noah," and "Jesus Fed the 5,000." If you have a favorite Bible story you heard as a kid, share it with your preschooler. Additionally, use the following biblical concept statements and suggested activities to teach your child the Bible.

Biblical Concept Statements

- Everything in the Bible is true.
- The Bible teaches us what God and Jesus are like.
- People wrote only God's words in the Bible.

- The Bible teaches that Jesus died on a cross but came back to life.
- The Bible teaches about right and wrong choices.

Bible-Learning Activities

The Bible teaches us what God and Jesus are like.

Ask your older preschooler, "What does God look like? What does Jesus look like? What color hair does God have? What color hair does Jesus have? Is Jesus tall or short?" State, "No one knows what God looks like; however, we do know that Jesus lived on the earth until He returned to heaven." Next, find some pictures of Jesus online or in your child's Bible. Continue, "Jesus lived on earth a long time ago, before phones with cameras, so we don't know what Jesus looks like. However, the Bible does teach us about God and Jesus. We know that God and Jesus love and care for us." Read or paraphrase these Bible verses that tell us what God and Jesus are like: John 15:9, 14; 1 Peter 5:7; and 1 John 4:10.

The Bible teaches about right and wrong choices.

Most four- and five-year-olds can differentiate between right and wrong choices. Play a game by asking your child to stand up if you state a right choice and sit down if you mention a wrong choice. Make statements such as these: "Obey your parents," "Yell at your brother/sister/friend," "Keep watching TV after your mother asks you to turn it off," "Help put dirty dishes in the sink or dishwasher," "Help fold clothes," and "Tell your parents something that is not true." Make up additional statements as long as your child shows interest. Sometimes your preschooler may give an opposite response to be silly or to get attention. Be sure to affirm your child when he chooses wisely.

Teaching Younger Elementary Kids about the Bible

Younger elementary kids are beginning to read, and some churches gift them with a full-text Bible. Seeing the excitement on children's faces and hearing it in their voices as they recognize and read words in the Bible is a wonderful thing for parents to experience. Take advantage of your child's eagerness to learn and instill biblical truth in their hearts and minds.

Biblical Concept Statements

- Bible truths never change.
- The Bible helps people know more about God, Jesus, and the Holy Spirit.
- God helped people know what to write in the Bible.
- The Bible teaches that Jesus died on a cross, was buried, and was raised from the dead.
- The Bible teaches how God wants people to live.

Bible-Learning Activities

Bible truths never change.

Read a few of the following verses with your child: Genesis 1:1, 27; 7:5, 10; Deuteronomy 5:22; Luke 2:7; 23:33; 24:6. After you read each verse, ask your child, "Did this really happen? Is it true?" Then say, "No matter what I read from this Bible, it is all true." As a family, begin to memorize these words: "All Scripture is inspired by God and is profitable for teaching, for rebuking, for correcting, for training in righteousness" (2 Tim. 3:16).

The Bible teaches that Jesus died on a cross, was buried, and was raised from the dead.

Gather paper and washable markers or colored pencils. Ask your child to help you make a list of all the things he knows about Jesus. List each fact on a sheet of paper. Remind your elementary child of Jesus' death on the cross and resurrection if they are not on the list. Next, guide your child to draw a picture of a cross on a separate piece of paper. Encourage him to make a list under the cross of what he knows about Jesus' death, burial, and resurrection. Refer to John 19:15–20:18 as needed. If your child expresses curiosity regarding why Jesus had to die, use "Appendix A: The Gospel, God's Plan for Me" as a discussion guide.

Teaching Middle Elementary Kids about the Bible

Many of your child's core beliefs about the Bible start to solidify during the middle elementary years. The following concept statements and activities will help ensure those beliefs are in accordance with God's Word.

Biblical Concept Statements

- Everything in the Bible is true and will last forever.
- The Bible is God's message about Himself.
- God inspired people to know what to write in the Bible.

- The Bible teaches that Jesus died on a cross, was buried, and was raised from the dead for the forgiveness of sins.
- The Bible teaches how to live a Christian life.

Bible-Learning Activities

God inspired people to know what to write in the Bible.

Gather two or three books in your house and ask your child who wrote each book. Mention that the people who wrote the books are often referred to as *authors*. Next, point to your child's Bible and ask who the author is. Point out that God is the author and He inspired, or told, many people to write the actual words we read in our Bible. Mention that the Bible actually consists of sixty-six books. Using online Bible reference tools, a Bible Dictionary, or a study Bible, guide your child to discover who wrote some of the books in the Bible. State, "While we may not know the names of all the Bible writers, we do know that the Bible is true because God is the author."

The Bible teaches how to live a Christian life.

You'll probably have this conversation more than once throughout your child's elementary, middle school, and high school years. Reassure your child that the Bible is not a rule book designed to make us miserable. Rather, the Bible tells us who God and Jesus are and what God and Jesus are like. Since we are to be like Jesus, the Bible teaches us how God wants us to live a Christian life. In fact, Paul says, "Adopt the same attitude as that of Christ Jesus" (Phil. 2:5). Guide your elementary student to make a list of how God wants us to live. Point out that God wants what is best for us.

Help your child realize that Christians should live differently than non-Christians.

Teaching Preteens about the Bible

By the time your child is a preteen, she may have developed a basic understanding of the Bible and biblical truth. Continue to encourage regular Bible reading, memorization, and life application. Give your preteen tools to defend their belief that the Bible is God's Word and is true from Genesis to Revelation.

Biblical Concept Statements

- The Bible is true, without error, and will last forever.
- The Bible is God's message about Himself and His salvation plan through Jesus.
- The Bible is the only inspired, written Word of God.
- The Bible teaches that salvation through Jesus is God's gift of forgiveness.
- The Bible teaches how to live a Christian life by following Jesus.

Bible Conversation Starters

The Bible is true, without error, and will last forever.

Read these Bible verses with your preteen and ask her to explain the meaning of each one: Psalm 119:89; Isaiah 40:8; and Mark 13:31. Talk with your child about what she believes regarding the Bible. If your preteen has difficulty clearly communicating that the Bible is true, spend some time helping her gain additional understanding. Start by pointing out that "the word of God is living and effective and sharper than any double-edged sword" (Heb. 4:12). You may want to do an apologetics study with your preteen to prepare her for the inevitable attacks to her biblical beliefs.

The Bible teaches how to live a Christian life by following Jesus.

Initiate a conversation with your preteen related to what the Bible teaches concerning living a Christian life by following Jesus. Mention that the Bible doesn't speak specifically to every issue your preteen will confront. However, the Bible does provide principles that help us know how to live. Read Ephesians 5:1–2 and talk about what it means to "be imitators of God." Remind your child that "if anyone is in Christ, he is a new creation" (2 Cor. 5:17). Talk about a recent choice your preteen made and if that decision was a reflection of being a new creation in Christ.

Teaching Middle Schoolers about the Bible

As I (Ken) put these words on the page, I am watching a popular award show that recognizes the best in the music industry. I listened as two or three of the winners gave thanks to God. Without sounding judgmental, I never felt any praise was really intended for God the Father. In fact, I had the overwhelming feeling that God the Father was brokenhearted over the overtly sinful presentation. Your middle schooler needs to know what the Bible teaches about today's pop cultural trends. Your child is watching, hearing, and participating in a variety of cultural experiences that are directly opposed to Scripture.

Biblical Concept Statements

- The Bible is true, without error, and will last forever.
- The Bible is the story of God's work in creation and centers around Jesus.
- The Bible is the only inspired written Word of God.
- Through the Bible, we know God Himself and how He expects us to live.

Bible Conversation Starters

The Bible is the story of God's work in creation and centers around Jesus.

Ask your middle schooler to describe the Bible. He may say something to the effect that the Bible is a collection of stories. Many adults would concur. However, the Bible is actually *one* story. From Genesis to Revelation, the Bible is the one story of God's redemptive plan found ultimately in Jesus. Explain to your middle schooler that God's message of redemption is basic to his biblical understanding and spiritual growth. Ask if he has questions related to this biblical truth. If so, take the time to respond with open-ended answers that continue the flow of conversation.

Through the Bible, we know God Himself and how He expects us to live.

Read Psalm 99 with your middle schooler; talk about what these nine verses reveal about God's character. Ask, "Since God is holy, how do you think God wants us to live?" Compassionately discuss biblical principles related to gender and sexuality, smoking and vaping, alcohol, porn, and cyberbullying. Ask, "Should Christians live differently than non-Christians?" Mention that the Bible says, "Do not be conformed to this age, but be transformed by the renewing of your mind, so that you may discern what is the good, pleasing, and perfect will of God" (Rom. 12:2).

Teaching High Schoolers about the Bible

Your high schooler needs the Bible, and she needs you to teach her biblical truths. Even though that task is difficult at times, be willing to get in your student's life and fight for her spiritual well-being. These days are unique and challenging. However, the truth in the Bible answers current societal questions. I (Ken) encourage you to engage your high schooler in face-to-face conversations (not via text) related to truths found only in the inspired Word of God, the Bible.

Biblical Concept Statements

- The Bible is internally consistent, God's truth, without error, totally trustworthy, and will last forever.
- The Bible is the story of God's work to redeem fallen creation through the saving work of Jesus, who will one day make all things new.
- The Bible consists of the sixty-six books of the Old and New Testaments and is the only inspired written Word of God.
- Through the Bible, we know God Himself, and we know how He expects us to live in order to follow Christ and experience His blessing.

Bible Conversation Starters

The Bible is internally consistent, God's truth, without error, totally trustworthy, and will last forever.

Many high schoolers enjoy a good debate. As a parent, you may feel that your child sometimes voices disagreement with you just for the sake of the argument. Take advantage of your student's propensity to argue by debating the trustworthiness of the Bible. In so doing, you'll be preparing him for real-life encounters now and after high school graduation. Inform your student that you will assume the posture of a skeptic, even though personally you believe the Bible is completely true. Have fun, while challenging your high schooler's beliefs. Ask questions such as, "Is the Bible a collection of morality tales? How do you know the Bible's teachings about Jesus are true? Can the theory of evolution and creationism coexist?" When you're ready, take time to debrief and assure your student of your true beliefs.

Through the Bible, we know God Himself, and we know how He expects us to live in order to follow Christ and experience His blessing.

Ask: "What do you think the Bible teaches about how God wants us to live?" Listen to what your student says as well as what he doesn't say. Read Romans 12:1–2 and ask your high schooler if the following options are things God wants us to do: choose our own gender identity, take illegal drugs or abuse prescription drugs, smoke or vape, drink alcohol, perform acts of self-harm such as cutting, look at porn, engage in sex outside of marriage, sext, and participate in cyberbullying. The list could go on and on. Your high schooler will have passionate opinions about each of these topics. Remind your student that while the Bible doesn't speak specifically to every current issue, the Bible does provide principles for Christian living.

Digging Deeper in Biblical Truth

Use the statements below to help your high schooler think deeply about the Bible and be prepared to defend his beliefs.

Being: As God's children, we are called to be like Jesus. The Bible reveals who Jesus is, and we grow to be more like Him as we understand and apply the truths found in the Scriptures.

Doing: Because we are transformed by the Bible, we should devote ourselves to regularly studying and applying the truths of Scripture.

Apologetic: Many claim that there are errors in Scripture or that the Bible contradicts itself in places. However, all Scripture is the Word of God, is without error, is trustworthy, and is transformative.

6

Teaching My Family Who God Is

I (Ken) was seven years old when I first experienced the epic movie, *The Ten Commandments*, starring Charlton Heston. I was totally amazed visually, and the most enthralling aspect was the voice of the actor representing God. The massive, deep voice speaking to Moses compelled me to listen intently. That evening, the Lord planted seeds in my seven-year-old heart and mind related to the awesome power of God Almighty. Today, I am still doing my best to share with others the life-changing power of God the Father.

What about you? Does the thought of teaching your kids about the Holy God who is all-powerful, all-knowing, and present everywhere at all times in all places overwhelm you? If you answered, "Yes," stop and take a deep breath. Determine to enjoy the exciting adventure of teaching your child about God. The process of discipleship and spiritual growth will take time, and the Holy Spirit will empower you throughout the journey.

Read the Bible

Why is Bible reading important? Preschoolers and children will begin to understand that what you are teaching them about God is based on God's truth. As your preteens and teens observe you personally reading, studying, and meditating on Scripture, they will watch to see if your life reflects God's love.

Encourage your child to read Deuteronomy 6:4–5 with you. These words that Moses spoke to the Hebrews is known as the Shema (shuh MAH), which means, "hear." The Shema is "the main statement of the Jewish law that says God is the one true God and His people are commanded to love and obey Him."[1] When asked about the most important commandment, Jesus answered, "The most important is 'Listen, Israel! The Lord our God, the Lord is one. Love the Lord your God with all your heart, with all your soul, with all your mind, and with all your strength.' The second is, 'Love your neighbor as yourself.' There is no other command greater than these" (Mark 12:29–31).

Think about the Bible

How should the Shema impact your parenting or teaching? What do these verses tell us about God? Ask your child, "How big is God?" While none of us can fully comprehend the vastness of God, our response to Who God is should always be to love Him with all of our being.

Teaching Younger Preschoolers about God

God is so big. Use the following statements and activities to begin the process of helping your preschooler gain valuable knowledge related to God.

Biblical Concept Statements

- God is good.
- God made me.
- God loves me.
- God hears me.
- God helps me.
- God loves people.

Bible-Learning Activities

God is good.

Give your child their favorite snack food. Talk about how the snack is good. Explain that a lot of things in your preschooler's young life are considered good, including God. However, God is a different kind of good because He is Creator, all-powerful, all-knowing, and God is everywhere. State, "God is good and is better than our favorite snack. God is better than anyone and anything."

God loves me.

Gather paper, crayons or markers, and scissors. Instruct your preschooler to fold the paper in half. Next, cut the shape of a half heart. Hand the half heart to your preschooler and allow her to open the paper revealing the heart. Share that this heart helps us remember that God loves us. Use the crayon or marker and allow your child to write her name on the heart. Place the heart in a highly visible location in your home. Every time you walk by the heart, remind your child that God loves her.

Teaching Middle Preschoolers about God

How should we approach teaching middle preschoolers about God and that He is good, He made us, and He loves us? Here are a few helpful suggestions.

Biblical Concept Statements

- God is good to me.
- God made everything.
- God loves people and is with them.
- God hears me when I pray.
- God helps people.
- God shows His love to me.
- God loves me even when I make wrong choices.
- God tells me to sing and pray to Him.
- God tells me to do what He says.
- God can do anything.
- God does what He says He will do.
- God knows everything about me.
- God is real.

Bible-Learning Activities

God is good to me.

Play a simple rhythm game by clapping while repeating the phrase, "God is good," several times. Pause, then play again saying, "God is good. He made _____ [your child's name]." Pause and encourage your preschooler to fill in the blank. Continue playing until your child begins to lose interest. Say, "God is good. God made everything."

God made everything.

Locate a picture of your family. Guide your preschooler to identify the people in the photograph, along with anything else in the picture, such as grass, trees, or animals. Each time your preschooler names a person or item, state, "God made _____ [your child's response]." Say, "God made you, and God made everything." Encourage your child to look in a mirror. Say, "God made _____ [child's name]." Lead your preschooler to pray a simple thank-you prayer for all the people and things God has made.

God loves me even when I make wrong choices.

Looking in your preschooler's eyes, say, "I love you when you are awake; I love you when you are asleep; I love you when you are at home; and I love you when you go to _____ [preschool, grandparent's house, etc.]." Then mention that sometimes we make wrong choices. Prompt your child to identify some wrong choices he has made. Assure him that God loves us all the time, even when we make wrong choices.

Teaching Older Preschoolers about God

How should you approach teaching your older preschooler about God and the fact that He is good, He created everything, and He is always with us? Use the following statements and suggestions to get started.

Biblical Concept Statements

- God is good to everyone.
- God created everything.
- God is always with people.
- God hears people pray.
- God helps and provides for people.
- God shows His love to people.
- God loves people even when they make wrong choices.
- God tells people to worship Him.
- God tells people to obey Him.
- God can do all things.
- God always keeps His promises.
- God knows everything.
- God is real and true.

Bible-Learning Activities

God created everything.

Locate a basket, bucket, or paper bag. Share that you are going on a creation walk to look for things God created. Collect some of these things on a walk around your home or outside. Referring to Genesis, chapter 1, challenge your older preschooler to sort the items by the day God created them. Remind your child that God created everything.

God hears people pray.

Lead your preschooler in a simple listening activity. Start by asking your preschooler to sit in a chair. Explain that you are going to say a simple phrase and then they will repeat what you say. Say,

"God hears people pray." Allow your preschooler to repeat what you said. Move a short distance from your preschooler and repeat the phrase. Now, move to another room and repeat the phrase. Make sure your preschooler can still hear what you are saying. Return to your child and offer her a snack. State, "You heard me talk to you, even when I went to another room. God hears people pray to Him anytime and anywhere." Lead your preschooler to thank God for her snack.

God knows everything.

Ask your preschooler to count the number of individual hairs on your head. Before long, your child will give up. Read Matthew 10:30 and mention that God knows exactly how many hairs each of us has. If you happen to be in a location where there is sand, you could ask your older preschooler to count the individual grains of sand. Mention that only God knows the number of hairs on your head and the number of grains of sand on the beach or in the sandbox. Pray, thanking God that He knows everything about everything.

Teaching Younger Elementary Kids about God

How should you approach teaching your younger elementary child about God and His perfection, that He is the Creator and worthy to be praised, and that He is everywhere? As a starting point, use the following statements and suggested activities.

Biblical Concept Statements

- God is perfect.
- God is Creator and worthy to be praised.

- God is everywhere.
- God hears and answers prayer.
- God helps and provides for His people.
- God shows love to His people.
- God loves people enough to provide forgiveness for their wrong choices.
- God tells people to worship Him and to tell others about Him.
- God expects people to obey, respect, and honor Him.
- God is powerful and in control of all things.
- God is fair and can be trusted.
- God knows all things.
- God is real, the only true God.
- God is the Father, the Son, and the Holy Spirit.

Bible-Learning Activities

God is Creator and worthy to be praised.

Read Genesis 1:1 and help your child memorize it. She probably enjoys using her "outside voice" indoors, so encourage your child to shout the verse. Then as a contrast, lead her to recite the verse with a softer voice. Point out that God created the world in six days and is worthy to be praised. Ask, "How can we give God praise for the things He has made for us to enjoy?" Guide your child to find an item that God created. Together, examine the item and talk about what makes it unique. Suggest your child pray, praising God for His creation.

God is powerful and in control of all things.

Ask your child to name things that are powerful. If he mentions superheroes, try to redirect his thinking to examples that are real. Talk about the power of water rushing in a river, waves crashing in the ocean, wind blowing across a field, and a lion roaring in the savannah. Suggest your child draw something powerful. Ask: "Do things that are powerful sometimes frighten you?" The next time your child is afraid, encourage him to remember that God is more powerful than anything we can imagine. Moreover, God is also in control of everything.

Teaching Middle Elementary Kids about God

What is the best approach for teaching eight- and nine-year-olds about God and that He is perfect, He is the Creator and worthy to be praised, and He is everywhere? Start by using the following concept statements and Bible-learning activities.

Biblical Concept Statements

- God is holy.
- God is Creator and worthy to be praised.
- God is everywhere at all times.
- God knows what people need and desire, but still expects them to pray.
- God has concern and care for all people.
- God loves and values people around the world.
- God proved His unconditional love for people by sending Jesus.
- God is worthy of worship.

- God deserves respect, obedience, and honor.
- God is all-powerful and in control of all things.
- God is faithful and just.
- God is all-knowing.
- God has always been, and always will be.
- God is God the Father, God the Son, and God the Holy Spirit (the Trinity).

Bible-Learning Activities

God loves and values people around the world.

Did your parents ever say something to the effect of, "You're not the only person in the world"? I (Ken) heard that many times growing up. Kids tend to think the world revolves around them. Our job is to teach them the world revolves around our Creator. God is at the center of all creation, and He loves and values all people. Locate a few pictures of people from other nations. While looking at the pictures with your child, talk about where each person lives. State, "God loves and values all people, whether they live next door or on the other side of the world."

God proved His unconditional love for people by sending Jesus.

Ask your child, "Do you know how much God loves you?" Tell her that God loves her so much that He sent His one and only Son, Jesus, to die for everyone including her. Ask your child if she can think of a way to make God stop loving her. Say, "God loves you unconditionally, which means there is nothing you can do that will cause God to stop loving you." If you sense that your child is ready to talk more about God's love and our response, refer to "Appendix A: The Gospel, God's Plan for Me."

Teaching Preteens about God

Teaching your preteen about God is an exciting adventure that will not be accomplished in one day. Use the following concept statements and conversation starters over time to fuel your older child's spiritual growth.

Biblical Concept Statements

- God is holy and perfect.
- God, the Creator, is to be worshiped, not His creations.
- God is omnipresent—He is everywhere at all times.
- God hears people's prayers and communicates with them.
- God has concern and care for all people no matter their status, race, or ethnicity.
- God loves and values people around the world no matter their status, race, or ethnicity.
- God proved His unconditional love for people through the sacrifice of Jesus the Christ.
- God expects people to worship Him with all their hearts, souls, minds, and strength.
- God deserves respect, obedience, and honor. God wants us to live for His glory.
- God is omnipotent—He is all-powerful, sovereign, and good.

- God is righteous.
- God is omniscient—He is all-knowing.
- God is eternal.
- God reveals Himself to us as God the Father, God the Son, and God the Holy Spirit (the Trinity).

Bible Conversation Starters

God is holy and perfect.

Ask your preteen, "Do you know of anything that is perfect?" Point out that the only thing or living being that is perfect is God. People are not perfect because of sin. Our world is broken because of sin, but we live with hope because our God is holy and perfect. The Bible teaches that while we are not perfect, our goal is to become more like Jesus who *is* perfect. Read 1 Peter 1:15–16 and talk about ways we can be holy and more like Jesus.

God is omniscient—He is all knowing.

Ask your preteen, "Who is the smartest person you know? What makes that person smart? What is the name of someone else who is smart? Why do you think that person is smart?" Explain that the Bible teaches God is omniscient, which means God knows everything about everything and is more knowledgeable than the smartest person on the planet. Ask your child for some examples of what God knows, such as the number of grains of sand on all the beaches in the world, how many birds fly in the sky, the number of stars and planets in space, how much water is in all of the world's oceans, and how many blood cells are in your body. God knows the answers to all of these questions and more!

Teaching Middle Schoolers about God

Your middle schooler is experiencing massive changes which can affect body image and self-confidence. Help your young teen navigate the transition from childhood to adulthood. Continue to be her primary spiritual influencer. Use the following statements and suggestions to point your student to our perfect Father who longs for her identity to be found in Christ.

Biblical Concept Statements

- Because God is holy, He is altogether separate from and far above people who are sinful.
- God is Creator, all creation is a result of His work, and people were created to live in relationship with Him.
- God is omnipresent (all places at all times), omniscient (all-knowing), and omnipotent (all-powerful).
- God communicates to us through His Word and hears and answers when we pray.
- God relates to His people according to His covenant promises, He is faithful, and He always keeps His promises to us.
- God is loving and righteous and will one day make right all that sin has damaged.
- God is worthy of our worship because of how He relates to us and because of who He is, and we owe to Him our attention and affections.

- God (Father, Son, and Holy Spirit) is eternal, and has existed for eternity past and will exist for eternity into the future.
- There is one God who reveals Himself to us as Father, Son, and Holy Spirit.

Bible Conversation Starters

God communicates to us through His Word and hears and answers when we pray.

Ask your teen, "When was the last time you read your Bible? What did you read? What did reading your Bible teach you about God? Did God speak to you about anything? What have you been praying about lately?" These questions can open a conversation with your teen that will allow you to share that God communicates to us through His Word and hears and answers when we pray. If your child has been neglecting the spiritual disciplines of Bible reading and prayer, try to understand why and gently help him develop a plan to spend more time with God.

God relates to His people according to His covenant promises, He is faithful, and He always keeps His promises to us.

Has someone disappointed your young teen recently? Perhaps a friend? Maybe a teacher, coach, or student pastor? Even you might be the cause of your child's disappointment. When your teen is hurt and brokenhearted, your encouragement as a parent is critical. Listen with empathy to your child without immediately trying to fix the situation. Acknowledge and validate his feelings. When he's ready, gently remind your teenager that there is One who never disappoints us and always keeps His promises. Encourage your child with these words of our faithful, loving Heavenly Father: "Haven't I commanded you: be strong and courageous? Do not be afraid or discouraged, for the LORD your God is with you wherever you go" (Josh. 1:9).

Teaching High Schoolers about God

Your role as a parent is beginning to transition from supervisor to guide, and your high schooler has an amazing ability to understand complex biblical concepts about God. Look for opportunities to disciple your teenager as you use the statements and Bible conversation starters, below. Enjoy the ensuing discussions. Yes, they may occur at midnight, on the sofa, in the car, or at the kitchen counter. However, your student will treasure these discussions in the years ahead.

Biblical Concept Statements

- Because God is holy, He is altogether separate from and infinitely above people who are sinful, and He deserves our reverence and obedience.
- God is Creator, all creation is a result of His work, and He created people in His image and as His crowning achievement to enjoy a relationship with Him and reflect His glory.
- God is omnipresent (all places at all times), omniscient (all-knowing), and omnipotent (all-powerful), and exercises sovereignty over all creation.

- God communicates to us through His Word and hears and answers when we pray, and our spiritual maturity depends on these spiritual disciplines.
- God relates to His people according to His covenant promises, and even though we are not always faithful to Him, God keeps His promises and always has and always will be faithful to us.
- God is loving and righteous, grieves the impact of sin on the world, and will one day make right all that sin has damaged.
- God is worthy of our worship, and to misplace attention or affections to worldly things which are rightly owed to God is idolatry.
- God (Father, Son, and Holy Spirit) is eternal, and although He is not bound by time, He chooses to operate in it in order to relate to us.
- There is one eternal God who reveals Himself to us as Father, Son, and Holy Spirit, and each person of the Trinity has distinct personal attributes.

Bible Conversation Starters

Because God is holy, He is altogether separate from and infinitely above people who are sinful, and He deserves our reverence and obedience.

As you listen for the opportunity to influence and disciple your teenager, ask questions such as, "How is God different from man? How does our sin separate us from God? How can you as a teenager show reverence to God when your friends don't? How are you being obedient to God right now?" These questions can and will influence many conversations in the coming months.

God is worthy of our worship, and to misplace attention or affections to worldly things which are rightly owed to God is idolatry.

Read Exodus 20:3–4 and ask your teenager, "What does it mean to 'not have other gods besides' the One True God? How does God's command to 'not make an idol' apply to us today? How serious is God regarding idolatry? What are some things your friends place before God? Would you consider those things to be idols? Why or why not?" Without sounding judgmental, remind your child that God is worthy of worship, and any misplaced attention or affection is idolatry.

Digging Deeper in Biblical Truth

Use the statements below to help your high schooler think deeply about God and be prepared to defend his beliefs.

Being: All people are created in God's image to reflect Him and live in relationship with Him. Sin damaged that image and brought separation, but Christians are new creations with the distinct privilege of enjoying restored relationships with God and reflecting His character to the world in a special way.

Doing: Because we are created to reflect God and live in relationship with Him, we should continually pursue God in His Word and through prayer, live in continual fellowship within the church, and evangelize those who do not know Him.

Apologetic: Many today believe there are many gods and many ways to heaven, and that we are free to define God according to our personal perspectives. However, Scripture teaches there is one God with only one way to heaven through trust in His only Son, Jesus. God Himself defines who He is and not people.

7

Teaching My Family Who Jesus Is

I (Ken) love Christmas! I love all of the Christmas traditions. I love the sights of ornaments and lights on trees. I love Christmas music. I love homemade candies and baked goods. I love wrapping and receiving gifts. I love candles in the window. I love sending and receiving Christmas cards. But do you know what I love most about Christmas? Telling people about the birth of Jesus.

Christmas is one of the two times the world is still willing to look to the church for biblical truth. (The other is Easter.) Hearts are warm to hearing the biblical truths related to Jesus and His birth. How can you and your family share the life-changing message of Jesus with others? Consider displaying a nativity set in your yard, home, or office. Use the nativity scene as a conversation starter about Jesus. I (Ken) have a few conversation starters that I display at Christmas. As a collector, I have more than 1,000 nativity sets from all over the world that I display year after year. Why? So, I can tell people, especially children, about Jesus.

Teaching our kids about Jesus is a year-long endeavor and not just something we do at Christmas and Easter. (Christmas carols in the summer, anyone?) In this chapter we dive into suggestions for discipling preschoolers, children, preteens, middle schoolers, and high schoolers and teaching them about Jesus. Get ready, this is going to be a blast for you and your entire family!

Read the Bible

The entire Bible, from the first page to the last, points to the supremacy of Jesus. Read Genesis 3:14–15; Isaiah 9:6; Luke 2:25–35, 46–52; John 1:1–5; Colossians 1:15–20; and Revelation 22:13. These are just a few of the Scripture passages that indicate God the Father's redemptive plan has always been found in God the Son, Jesus.

Think about the Bible

Who is Jesus? That is a difficult question. None of us can comprehend fully how Jesus is simultaneously 100 percent man and 100 percent God when He walked on the earth. Perhaps the best place to start when responding to that question is to think about Jesus' impact on our daily lives. If you cannot think of ways Jesus makes a difference in your thoughts and actions, ask God to draw you into a closer relationship with Jesus.

Teaching Younger Preschoolers about Jesus

How should you approach teaching your young preschooler about Jesus? How do you help your child with a very limited vocabulary begin to understand that Jesus was born in a very different place and time, that God chose a family for Jesus, and that

Jesus grew just like your preschooler is growing? Following are a few helpful suggestions.

Biblical Concept Statements

- Jesus was born.
- God chose a family for Jesus.
- Jesus grew like me.
- Jesus learned about God.
- Jesus told people about God.
- Jesus helped people because He loved them.
- Jesus loves me.
- Jesus did everything God told Him to do.
- Jesus is alive.

Bible-Learning Activities

Jesus was born and God chose a family for Jesus.

Locate a non-breakable, realistic nativity set and remove the wise men. Invite your young preschool to explore the nativity figures. Read Luke 2:7, pointing to the words. Talk about Baby Jesus. Mention that God chose a family for Jesus. His mother's name was Mary, and His daddy's name was Joseph. If your child is like most children this age, he will carry one or two figures around the house or in the car. That's great, because you'll have additional opportunities to talk about Jesus' birth.

Jesus loves me.

Teach your younger preschooler this simple biblical truth by singing the old song, "Jesus Loves Me." If you are unfamiliar with the lyrics and tune, listen to the song via a mobile app with your child. Sing as you snuggle on the couch, as your preschooler dresses, as your child takes a bath, and as you drive in the car.

> *Jesus loves me, this I know*
> *For the Bible tells me so*
> *Little ones to Him belong*
> *They are weak, but He is strong*
> *Yes, Jesus loves me*
> *Yes, Jesus loves me*
> *Yes, Jesus loves me*
> *The Bible tells me so*

There is no better way to teach this biblical concept to your child than to make singing these words part of your daily rhythm.

Teaching Middle Preschoolers about Jesus

Your middle preschooler is probably beginning to sense that Jesus is special and may even say Jesus' name when prompted. Use the name of Jesus often as you teach your child the following biblical concepts.

Biblical Concept Statements

- God sent Jesus to earth.
- Angels told Mary and Joseph that Jesus would be born.
- Jesus grew like me and had a family.
- Jesus learned about God by reading the Scriptures.
- Jesus taught people about what God is like.
- Jesus healed sick people.
- Jesus loves people.

- Jesus is God's Son.
- Jesus always obeyed God.
- Jesus is with God.

Bible-Learning Activities

Angels told Mary and Joseph that Jesus would be born.

Locate an age-suitable nativity set that your preschooler can hold in her hands as you share this biblical truth. Make sure the figures are realistic in order to reinforce the fact that the stories in the Bible are about real people. Talk about Mary and Joseph, what their daily lives would have been like, and how our lives are both similar and different. Pick up the angel and share that angels told Mary and Joseph that Jesus would be born. Allow your preschooler to place the nativity pieces in and around the scene, even if the donkey lands on top of the stable!

Jesus healed sick people.

Gather a baby doll and some adhesive bandages. (You can make your own by placing a small cotton ball on a piece of masking tape and adhering the "bandage" to waxed paper.) As your child places the "bandages" on the doll, guide your child to recall a time he was sick. Read Luke 4:40 and explain that Jesus healed sick people.

Teaching Older Preschoolers about Jesus

While we know very little about Jesus as a young boy, we do know from Luke 2:52 that Jesus grew in much the same way your own child is growing. Kids this age love to learn new things, so enjoy teaching your older preschooler about Jesus.

Biblical Concept Statements

- God sent Jesus to earth as a real person.
- People in the Old Testament told that Jesus would be born.
- Jesus grew, learned, and had friends.
- Jesus prayed to God.
- Jesus taught people what God is like by what He said and did.
- Jesus performed miracles.
- People can obey Jesus because they love Him.
- Jesus died on the cross and then came back to life.
- Jesus is God's one and only Son.
- Jesus was tempted to sin.
- Jesus is in heaven with God.

God sent Jesus to earth as a real person.

Gather a baby doll, toy bottle, and baby blanket. Allow your older preschooler to hold the baby doll and pretend to care for it. Ask your older preschooler to share what he knows about Jesus. State: "Jesus was born in Bethlehem as a real baby. Jesus was a real person just like you are a real person. Mary and Joseph took care of Baby Jesus in much the same way you are taking care of your 'baby.'" Pray, thanking God that Jesus came to earth as a real person.

Jesus is in heaven with God.

Weather permitting, take your older preschooler on a walk outside. Looking up, say, "Jesus is in heaven with God." Ask: "Where is heaven?" Explain that we can't see heaven and don't know where it is; however, the Bible talks about heaven as being above the sky. Reference Acts 1:9–11 and mention that Jesus and God are in heaven.

Teaching Younger Elementary Kids about Jesus

As your younger elementary child makes friends outside of church, she may start hearing Jesus' name irreverently spoken as a swear word. Or, perhaps your child has a friend whose name is *Jesús*. The following concept statements and activities can help you teach your child that the Jesus of the Bible is God the Son and is worthy of our worship.

Biblical Concept Statements

- Jesus was God in human form.
- Prophets in the Old Testament told that Jesus would be born. Jesus is the Messiah who fulfilled Old Testament prophecies.
- Jesus understands what it is like to be human.
- Jesus worshiped God.
- Jesus taught through His life what God is like.
- Jesus raised people from the dead.
- People who love Jesus want to obey Him.
- Jesus died on the cross, and God raised Him from the dead.

- Jesus was sent to be my Savior.
- Jesus was tempted but did not sin.
- Jesus ascended to heaven but promised He would return one day.
- Jesus was with God at creation.

Bible-Learning Activities

Prophets in the Old Testament told that Jesus would be born. Jesus is the Messiah who fulfilled Old Testament prophecies.

Ask your child: "What is a prophet?" Explain that in the Bible prophets told people messages from God. Sometimes the messages were about God's Son who would come to earth one day. Read Isaiah 9:6 with your elementary student. Ask: "Who do you think Isaiah is talking about in this verse?" Explain that Isaiah was a prophet who lived a long time ago and who told people that one day a Savior would be born. That Savior was Jesus, born in Bethlehem just as another prophet Micah foretold (Mic. 5:2).

Jesus died on the cross, and God raised Him from the dead.

Gather two craft sticks, washable glue, and sand. Help your child make a cross by gluing the two craft sticks perpendicularly. Guide your elementary student to put glue on the cross-shaped craft sticks. Sprinkle sand on the glue and let dry before shaking off excess sand. For less of a mess, use glitter glue instead of sand. As young artistic hands are at work, talk about Jesus's death on the cross and how Jesus came back to life. Emphasize that Jesus is alive! Encourage your child to say a thank-you prayer to God for Jesus when he sees his completed craft.

Teaching Middle Elementary Kids about Jesus

Sometimes we forget the importance of Jesus' name. Use the statements and activities below to teach your child that, "God highly exalted him [Jesus] and gave him the name that is above every name, so that at the name of Jesus every knee will bow—in heaven and on earth and under the earth—and every tongue will confess that Jesus Christ is Lord, to the glory of God the Father" (Phil. 2:9–11).

Biblical Concept Statements

- Jesus was born of a virgin.
- God planned for Jesus to be the Savior from the beginning of time.
- Jesus is fully God and fully man.
- Jesus taught that worship is focused on God.
- Jesus taught about faith, trust, and obedience to God.
- Jesus performed miracles through the power of God.
- People can obey Jesus as a response to His love.
- Jesus died to pay the penalty for sin.
- Jesus is the Messiah and Savior.
- Jesus was human but resisted temptation.
- Jesus ascended to heaven but promised He would return one day.
- Jesus is eternal.

Bible-Learning Activities

Jesus died to pay the penalty for sin.

By now, your eight- or nine-year-old may know the story of Jesus' death, burial, and resurrection. However, your elementary student may not understand *why* Jesus had to die on the cross. When you sense that your child is ready for that conversation, start by reading Romans 3:23 together. Talk about the word, *all*. All means all! Everyone has sinned. In fact, we're born as sinners. Explain that sin consists of "actions, attitudes, words, or thoughts that do not please God."[1] Point out that the Bible has this to say about sin: "For the wages of sin is death, but the gift of God is eternal life in Christ Jesus our Lord" (Rom. 6:23). Explain that *wages* is another word for *payment*. Death is the payment for our sin. However, Jesus died on the cross to pay for our sin so we wouldn't have to. Through Jesus, God offers us the free gift of eternal life. As long as your child is interested, continue the conversation using "Appendix A: The Gospel, God's Plan for Me" as a guide.

Jesus was human but resisted temptation.

Encourage your child to list things that he is tempted to do that he knows are wrong. Give him the option to keep his list private. Next, ask: "Was Jesus ever tempted to do the wrong thing? Do you think Jesus ever committed a sin? Did Jesus resist the temptation of sin?" Listen for their answer. Now, read Matthew 4:1–11 with your elementary student. The Bible says that Jesus indeed was tempted because he was human, but He resisted the temptation to sin. Jesus "did not know sin" (2 Cor. 5:21). Jesus is different from us. Jesus is perfect and never, ever sinned (see Heb. 4:15).

Teaching Preteens about Jesus

As you navigate the preteen years with your child, your almost-teenager's Christian maturity will grow into their own faith. That is an exciting process to witness. The following biblical truths about Jesus will support your preteen throughout this process and will help you as the parent have a framework for daily conversations.

Biblical Concept Statements

- Jesus was born of a virgin.
- God planned for Jesus to be the Savior from the beginning of time and sent Jesus to earth at the perfect time.
- Jesus is fully God and fully man who came to earth in human form.
- Jesus taught that worship is for God's glory.
- Jesus taught that He is the only way to God.
- Jesus performed miracles because He is God's Son.
- Jesus transformed people through His love.
- Jesus' crucifixion, burial, and resurrection were a necessary part of God's plan for the forgiveness of sin.
- God sent Jesus to fulfill His promise of redemption.
- Jesus is holy and perfect.
- Jesus sits at God's right hand and intercedes for us as our advocate, mediator, and high priest. When Jesus returns, all things will be made new.
- Jesus has always existed and will always be with God.

Bible Conversation Starters

Jesus was born of a virgin.

Ask your preteen, "What made Jesus' birth unique, unlike the birth of anyone who lived before or after Jesus came to earth." Comment that when Jesus was born in Bethlehem, Mary His mother was a virgin. While you may be tempted to avoid the subject, many preteens already know (or think they know) what a virgin is. Explain that Mary was a virgin because she had not slept with Joseph or any other man. Read Luke 1:26–38 and talk about how Jesus' being born to a virgin gives proof to the Bible's claim that Jesus is God's Son.

Jesus has always existed and will always be with God.

Ask your preteen what the word *eternal* means. Be ready to coach your child that if something is eternal, it will last or exist forever. In addition, eternal things have no beginning and no ending. Encourage your almost-teenager to list things that will last forever. Read Revelation 21:1 and explain that nothing will exist forever; however, God is eternal—God the Father, God the Son, and God the Holy Spirit *are* eternal. We often place so much emphasis on Jesus' birth that we fail to recognize Jesus was present at creation, which means that Jesus has always existed (see John 1:1–3). In fact, Jesus Himself proclaims in Revelation 22:13, "I am the Alpha and the Omega, the first and the last, the beginning and the end." (The first and last letters of the Greek alphabet are alpha and omega, respectively.) Jesus existed before God created the world, and Jesus will live forever and ever.

Teaching Middle Schoolers about Jesus

Your middle schooler needs Jesus—at home, at school, on the ball field, on the stage, at a friend's house, and on social media. The following are a few suggestions that might help navigate the middle school years as you expand your child's head and heart knowledge about Jesus.

Biblical Concept Statements

- Jesus was conceived by the Holy Spirit and born of a virgin.
- From the beginning, God planned that Jesus would save people from their sins and sent Him at exactly the right time.
- Jesus is fully God and fully man, and He is altogether holy.
- Jesus lived for the glory of the Father and taught that we should do the same through lives of worship.
- Jesus is the only way people can connect with God.
- Because Jesus is God, He had the power to perform miracles.
- Jesus sits at God's right hand and continually prays for us.
- Jesus will one day return to exercise His reign over creation.

Bible Conversation Starters

Jesus was conceived by the Holy Spirit and born of a virgin.

Read Luke 1:26–38 with your middle schooler. In an effort not to embarrass your teenager, make sure he or she knows the meaning of the terms *conceived* and *virgin*. After a few minutes of discussion, ask, "How was it possible for Mary to conceive (become pregnant) if she had never had sex with a man?" The answer is simply stated in Luke 1:27: "For nothing will be impossible with God." In order for Jesus to be fully God and fully man, He had to be born of a virgin. Otherwise, Jesus would have been a person like us, the result of sexual relations between a man and a woman.

Jesus is fully God and fully man, and He is altogether holy.

Your middle schooler is normal if he has difficulty understanding this biblical concept. Jesus is both fully divine and fully human, yet one person, all at the same time. That sounds complicated to our finite minds. So, here are a few Bible verses that might help your young teenager begin to grasp this reality: Isaiah 9:6; Luke 1:35; John 1:1–5, 14; and Colossians 1:13–23. Pray with your student, asking God for wisdom to understand who Jesus is.

Teaching High Schoolers about Jesus

I (Ken) imagine that your high schooler has a fairly good understanding of Jesus. He or she can navigate many facts about who Jesus is, His purpose, and why He came to earth, but does your student know and understand how to apply these biblical truths to daily conversations with friends and teammates? The following suggestion should offer some help as you help your child navigate the high school experience.

Biblical Concept Statements

- Jesus was conceived by the Holy Spirit and born of a virgin, which means He did not inherit the sinful nature passed down from Adam, which made Him fit to be our Savior.
- From the beginning, God planned that Jesus would save people from their sins, and it was necessary that He would be crucified and raised.
- Jesus is fully God and fully man, and despite being tempted while on earth, remained altogether free from sin.
- Jesus lived for the glory of the Father and taught that we should do the same through lives of worship, service, and sacrifice.
- Because no sin can enter God's presence and because Jesus is holy, He is the only way people can connect with God.
- Jesus, because He is God, had the power to perform miracles, and He did so as a sign of His divine nature and to help people overcome their lack of faith.
- Jesus sits at God's right hand and continually intercedes for believers as our advocate, mediator, and High Priest. Jesus will one day return to exercise His reign over creation, and He will make all things new.

Bible Conversation Starters

Jesus lives for the glory of the Father and taught that we should do the same through lives of worship, service, and sacrifice.

Ask your high schooler what comments they have heard about the music at church. Most likely, your teenager has heard negative comments, such as, "The music is too loud; the music is not my style; we have to stand and sing too long; the songs are repetitive; we never sing the old hymns." The list could go on and on. The basis of the complaints is often personal preference; however, Jesus taught that true worship is directed toward and focused on God, not on ourselves. Jesus said, "The true worshipers will worship the Father in Spirit and in truth. Yes, the Father wants such people to worship him. God is spirit, and those who worship him must worship in Spirit and in truth" (John 4:23–24). Discuss with your student how worship is more than playing instruments and singing. Worship is living our lives in a way that honors and glorifies God the Father through service and sacrifice.

Jesus sits at God's right hand and continually intercedes for believers as our advocate, mediator, and High Priest. Jesus will one day return to exercise His reign over creation, and He will make all things new.

Drive somewhere with your high schooler. If your student is a licensed driver, let her drive and choose a destination—maybe a restaurant or coffee shop with patio seating, a park, or a hiking trail. Respect your teenager's potential desire not to be seen by her friends on your outing. Engage in a conversation about where Jesus is at the moment the two of you are talking. Mention that Jesus sits at God's right hand and is our intercessor, advocate, mediator, and High Priest. Talk about the meaning of those terms in the context of a personal relationship with Jesus. Ask your teen what emotions she experiences when she thinks about Jesus' return. Assure her that feeling apprehensive is normal, especially when we are young. Jesus' closest followers probably were anxious as well. Read John 14:1–4 and remind your student that Christians have nothing to fear about Jesus' return and reign. Focus on how Jesus will one day fix everything that sin has broken.

Digging Deeper in Biblical Truth

Use the statements below to help your high schooler think deeply about Jesus and be prepared to defend his beliefs.

Being: Because Jesus took our sin and, in its place, gave us His righteousness, though we were once separated from God, we are now accepted into God's presence.

Doing: Because Christianity necessarily involves following Christ, we should continually live in obedience to His commands as an expression of our faith in and love for Him.

Apologetic: Whereas many claim that Jesus was a good man or a great teacher, the truth is that Jesus is God.

8

Teaching My Family Who the Holy Spirit Is

Wait, don't skip this chapter! As a parent, you might feel that teaching your child about the concept of the Holy Spirit is a bit overwhelming. And, you probably are correct. However, you can handle it. Why? Because the Holy Spirit offers to give you the words to speak to your preschooler, elementary kid, preteen, middle schooler, or high school student.

Before embarking on this journey, ask yourself if your child is still literal minded. For example, when you say that you are having chocolate mousse for dessert, does your child envision a chocolate-covered moose with big antlers? Because preschoolers and younger elementary kids think more literally than they do abstractly, concentrate on teaching them foundational truths about God. As your child matures, introduce the more abstract concepts related to the Holy Spirit.

Read the Bible

The second verse of the Bible introduces the Holy Spirit: "Now the earth was formless and empty, darkness covered the surface of the watery depths, and the Spirit of God was hovering over the surface of the waters" (Gen. 1:2). While we may think about the Holy Spirit only within the context of the New Testament, God's Spirit was present at creation, and elsewhere in the Old Testament. Read Psalm 139:7–12; Isaiah 61:1–3; Matthew 1:18; John 14:16–17, 26; and Acts 1:8.

Think about the Bible

Talk with your elementary student, preteen, or teenager about the Holy Spirit's role in both the Old and New Testaments. Guide them to define who The Holy Spirit is. A helpful place to start might be something like this: "The Holy Spirit is the Spirit of God who helps people understand and accept God's plan of salvation. The Holy Spirit is the third Person of the Trinity—Father, Son, and Holy Spirit. Through the Holy Spirit, God acts to reveal His will, help Christians tell others about Jesus, and helps them know how to live in ways that please God. The Holy Spirit comes to live within those who trust Jesus as Savior and Lord."[1]

Teaching Younger Preschoolers about the Holy Spirit

Concept statements from the concept areas of God and Jesus lay a foundation for learning about the work of the Holy Spirit as your child grows. Following are examples of those biblical truths and ways to teach them to your young preschooler.

Biblical Concept Statements

- God helps me.
- God loves me.

Bible-Learning Activities

God helps me.

God is so helpful! How do you teach your young preschooler that God is helpful? Start by relating to your family with a servant attitude. As you serve your spouse and kids, it's important to remember that little eyes are watching. Babies and toddlers tend to mimic what they see their parents do. As you serve and help others, your preschoolers learn to do the same. When you see your child helping, encourage her with words of affirmation. Say, "You are a helper. God helps you and God helps me."

God loves me.

Speak the following in rhythm while clapping softly to a strong beat:

> God loves you, (Point to your child.)
> And God loves me. (Point to yourself.)
> God loves everything you see! (Raise your hands.)
> God helps you, (Point to your child.)
> And God helps me. (Point to yourself.)
> God helps everyone and me! (Raise your hands
> and then point to yourself.)

Teaching Middle Preschoolers about the Holy Spirit

Teaching middle preschoolers about the Holy Spirit is as simple as using biblical concept statements about God and Jesus. The following statements and activities help lay a foundation for future learning about the work of the Holy Spirit.

Biblical Concept Statements

- God helps people.
- God shows His love to people.
- God loves people and is with them.
- God shows His love to me.

Bible-Learning Activities

God loves people and is with them.

Ask your preschooler, "Can you see God? Why can't we see God? If we can't see God, does that mean God is still with us?" Point out that God is always with us even though we can't see him. Pointing to 1 John 4:10, say, "The Bible says, 'God loves us.'" Turn the pages of the Bible to Joshua 1:9 and point out that the Bible also says, "God is with me."

God shows His love to me.

Ask your preschooler, "How we can show that we love someone?" Next, ask your child how God shows His love for us. Comment, "God loves us in many ways. God gives us food to eat and juice to drink. God also loves us by listening when we pray and talk to Him." Lead your young child to pray, "Thank You, God, for loving me."

Teaching Older Preschoolers about the Holy Spirit

Older preschoolers are literal minded, so avoiding the use of analogies to describe the Holy Spirit is probably best. Instead, consider using biblical truths about God and Jesus to lay a foundation for learning about the work of the Holy Spirit when your child is older.

Biblical Concept Statements

- God helps and provides for people.
- God shows His love to people.
- God is always with people.

Bible-Learning Activities

God helps and provides for people.

Gather various vegetables and fruit, a vegetable scrubber or small dishcloth, and a dishpan with about two inches of water. Show your preschooler how to wash the vegetables and fruit. While your child works, say, "The Bible tells us God helps us and that 'God gives food to us'" (Ps. 136:25).

God shows His love to people.

Gather paper and washable markers. Ask your older preschooler, "How do you think God shows that He loves us?" Help your child begin to understand that God shows His love to people in many ways. Encourage your preschooler to draw a picture of ways God shows His love to us. You may want to provide ideas such as food to eat, clothes to wear, a place to live, and items in creation to enjoy.

Teaching Younger Elementary
Kids about the Holy Spirit

As you talk about simple biblical truths related to the Holy Spirit, be sensitive to your child's ability to understand abstract concepts. Use terms that your child may already know, such as *helper*.

Biblical Concept Statements

- The Holy Spirit is a special helper.
- The Holy Spirit helps people understand God's plan for salvation.
- The Holy Spirit helps people in times of trouble.
- The Holy Spirit has always worked in the world.
- The Holy Spirit helps Christians tell others about Jesus.
- The Holy Spirit helped people to write the Bible.
- God sent the Holy Spirit to help us know when we sin.

Bible-Learning Activities

The Holy Spirit is a special helper.

Ask your child to make a list of people who help others (police officers, firefighters, doctors, nurses, teachers, coaches, pastors, etc.). As your elementary student makes the list, talk about what each person does to help. Share with your child that the Holy Spirit is a special helper. State, "The Holy Spirit is with us all the time, everywhere we go, and is there to help us. How does the Holy Spirit help us? One way is to guide us in knowing how to make right decisions throughout our day."

God sent the Holy Spirit to help us know when we sin.

Ask the Holy Spirit to give you wisdom in knowing when to talk with your child about sin. How does your child know when they sin? They feel conviction. What is conviction? It is the bad feeling we have while we are committing a sin and after we have sinned. Where does this feeling come from? The Holy Spirit helps us know when we sin. Explain to your younger child that the Holy Spirit is always there to help us know when we have sinned and to prompt us to ask God to forgive us.

Teaching Middle Elementary Kids about the Holy Spirit

Teaching children about the Holy Spirit is a topic that needs careful attention. Pray and seek the Lord for wisdom as you share the following concepts with your child.

Biblical Concept Statements

- God, Jesus, and the Holy Spirit are the Trinity.
- The Holy Spirit urges people to receive God's salvation.
- The Holy Spirit is the Comforter.
- The Holy Spirit has worked and always will work in the world.
- The Holy Spirit helps Christians tell others about Jesus and God's plan.
- The Holy Spirit guided people to write God's words.
- The Holy Spirit convicts people of sin.

Bible-Learning Activities

The Holy Spirit is the Comforter.

As adults we don't enjoy talking about our mistakes and unwise choices, and neither do our kids. Be careful as you approach this conversation with your child. Talking with your elementary student about specific mistakes and wrong choices is more helpful than using generalities. The purpose of the conversation is to assist your child in learning from past behavior and to help him receive the comfort God provides through the Holy Spirit. Point out that the Holy Spirit provides comfort at other times, such as when a friend moves away, a grandparent dies, or a bully mistreats us.

The Holy Spirit helps Christians tell others about Jesus and God's plan.

Say to your elementary student, "Do you ever have a feeling that you are supposed to do something, but you don't know why? That could be the work of the Holy Spirit in your life." Talk about how the Holy Spirit may prompt us to tell others about Jesus and help us know the right words to speak. Discuss "Appendix A: The Gospel, God's Plan for Me" to ensure your child has the skills needed to share the message of salvation when the Holy Spirit nudges him or her to do so.

Teaching Preteens about the Holy Spirit

Your preteen is beginning to think and reason on her own. She also can think a bit more abstractly rather than just literally. Your child will now be able to grasp the fact that the Holy Spirit is with

Christians wherever they go. Enjoy the time you share with your preteen biblical truths related to the Holy Spirit.

Biblical Concept Statements

- The Trinity is eternal, holy, and perfect.
- The Holy Spirit is given to a person when he trusts Jesus as his Savior and Lord.
- God sent the Holy Spirit to be our Comforter.
- The Holy Spirit is eternal and active. The Holy Spirit intercedes for us.
- The Holy Spirit empowers Christians to tell others about Jesus and God's plan of salvation.
- The Holy Spirit inspired and guided people to write the Bible.
- The Holy Spirit pursues and convicts people of sin.

Bible Conversation Starters

The Holy Spirit is given to a person when he trusts Jesus as his Savior and Lord.

Read Acts 1:4–8 and Acts 2:1–4, 14–21. Ask your preteen, "Who sent the Holy Spirit? *(God the Father)*. Who received the gift of the Holy Spirit? *(Christians)*." State, "When we trust in Jesus as our personal Lord and Savior, the Holy Spirit comes to live inside us." Talk about the role of the Holy Spirit in the life of Christians. Ask your almost-teen if he has talked to a friend about Jesus and the words your child spoke seemed to come out of nowhere? Read Matthew 10:19–20 and comment that the Holy Spirit gives us the right words at the right time to tell people about Jesus. Mention that, among other things, the Holy Spirit convicts us of sin, comforts us, and guides us to make wise choices.

The Holy Spirit is eternal and active. The Holy Spirit intercedes for us.

Explain to your preteen that *intercede* means to do something or act on behalf of another person. The Bible says that when we don't know the words to pray or we're unable to pray, the Holy Spirit speaks to God the Father for us (see Rom. 8:26–27). That is one of the ways the Holy Spirit is active in our lives and in the lives of other Christians.

The Holy Spirit inspired and guided people to write the Bible.

Ask your child, "How did we get the Bible?" Allow them to answer and point out that the Holy Spirit inspired people and prompted them to write God's words that are in the Bibles we have today. Encourage your preteen to memorize 2 Peter 1:20–21 and use those verses in defense of the truthfulness of the Scriptures.

Teaching Middle Schoolers about the Holy Spirit

Your middle schooler is navigating a variety of emotions, pressures from their peers, and burdens related to life in general. I (Ken) want to encourage you to steadfastly support your middle schooler. Be present in his life. Listen more than you talk. Most importantly, continue to point him to biblical truth. A healthy discussion related to the purpose of the Holy Spirit in the Christian life might offer the comfort he needs.

Biblical Concept Statements

- God (Father, Son, and Holy Spirit) is eternal, and has existed for eternity past and will exist for eternity into the future.
- Each person who comes to faith in Christ receives the Holy Spirit and is given a spiritual gift.
- Jesus promised that God would send the Holy Spirit to minister to God's people in a special way.
- The Holy Spirit intercedes before the Father on our behalf.
- The Holy Spirit inspired and guided people to write the Bible.

Bible Conversation Starters

God (Father, Son, and Holy Spirit) is eternal, and has existed for eternity past and will exist for eternity into the future.

The Trinity—God the Father, God the Son, and God the Holy Spirit—has always been and always will be. It is that simple. But is it that simple for a middle schooler to understand? Maybe not. Spend some time with your middle schooler talking about eternity. How can our human minds even come close to understanding the meaning of how long eternity will be? Eternity is forever. That means there never was a time when God did not exist, and God will always exist. God has no beginning and no ending. Read the following Bible passages to reinforce this truth: Genesis 1:1–2; John 1:1–4; Colossians 1:15–17; Hebrews 1:10–12; 13:8; and Revelation 22:13.

Jesus promised that God would send the Holy Spirit to minister to God's people in a special way.

Read these Scripture passages with your middle schooler: Joel 2:28–29; Acts 2:1–4; 10:44–48; and 1 Corinthians 3:16; 12:13. Lead your student to list the special ways the Holy Spirit ministers to us as Christians. Ask how your student has personally experienced the Holy Spirit's work.

Teaching High Schoolers about the Holy Spirit

Yes, understanding the Holy Spirit is complicated. However, making sure your high school student understands the concept of the Holy Spirit is critical for his or her spiritual maturity. Now that you have made it to the high school years, wisely dive deeper into conversations related to spiritual things, including the work of the Holy Spirit.

Biblical Concept Statements

- God (Father, Son, and Holy Spirit) is eternal, and although He is not bound by time, He chooses to operate in it in order to relate to us.
- Each person who comes to faith in Christ receives the Holy Spirit and is endowed with a spiritual gift to be used to serve the church.
- Jesus promised that God would send the Holy Spirit, and the Spirit has come to convict, teach, comfort, lead, strengthen, and seal us, as well as to produce fruit within and through us.

- The Holy Spirit intercedes before the Father on our behalf when we do not know how or what to pray.
- The Holy Spirit inspired and guided people to write the Bible and used the personalities and voices of men to communicate the very words of God.

Bible Conversation Starters

Each person who comes to faith in Christ receives the Holy Spirit and is endowed with a spiritual gift to be used to serve the church.

Ask your high schooler, "Did you know that each person who trusts in Jesus as his Savior and Lord receives the Holy Spirit and is given a spiritual gift?" Read Galatians 5:22–26 and talk about what gift your student is drawn toward. Remind your child that the Holy Spirit gives us gifts to glorify God and to benefit the church. Ask: "How do you think God wants you to use your spiritual gift?" Next, read 1 Corinthians 13. Explain that love trumps everything. In other words, using spiritual gifts in the absence of love is considered misuse and does not honor God.

Jesus promised that God would send the Holy Spirit, and the Spirit has come to convict, teach, comfort, lead, strengthen, and seal us, as well as to produce fruit within and through us.

As a review, read these Bible passages with your high schooler: Joel 2:28–29; Acts 2:1–4; 10:44–48; and 1 Corinthians 3:16; and 12:13. Ask your high schooler if she knows that Jesus promised

God would send the Holy Spirit to convict, teach, comfort, lead, strengthen, and seal us, as well as to produce fruit within and through us. Share a specific example of how you have personally experienced the Holy Spirit working in one of these ways. Next, spend some time talking about fruit produced by the Holy Spirit. Read Luke 6:43–45 and Colossians 1:9–14. Pray with your student, asking the Holy Spirit to produce good fruit in and through you.

Digging Deeper in Biblical Truth

Use the statements below to help your high schooler think deeply about the Holy Spirit and be prepared to defend his beliefs.

Being: As members of God's family, we are filled with the Holy Spirit and have received from Him gifts to be used in serving the church. Exercising these gifts is a privilege and responsibility, and God works through us to impact others.

Doing: Because the Holy Spirit resides in the lives of all believers and has given us all a spiritual gift, we should work to discern that gift and then exercise it in building up the church.

Apologetic: Whereas many see the Holy Spirit as an energy or force, the truth is the Holy Spirit is a Person, coequal with the Father and the Son within the Trinity, and is Himself God.

9

Teaching My Family How to Love People

The beloved Peanuts® comic strip character, Linus, is credited with saying, "I love mankind; it's people I can't stand."[1] Definitely not a biblical statement, but a sentiment many of us have from time to time. Theoretically we love humanity, but in practice our attitudes and actions toward people are often contrary to biblical teaching.

Read the Bible

What does the Bible say about people and our treatment of others? Read Genesis 1:26–27; Matthew 5:43–44; Mark 12:29–31; and James 3:9. God created people in His image, making us different from all the other created beings. In fact, God places such a high value on people "that while we were still sinners, Christ died for us" (Rom. 5:8).

Think about the Bible

The Bible turns Linus's statement on its head, doesn't it? When we get so frustrated with people that we want to pack our bags and sail to a deserted island, we turn our backs on what the Bible teaches about our relationships with others. When we are unkind to the next-door neighbor with the barking dog, we are mistreating God's most prized creation. When we criticize the slow driver in front of us, we are complaining about an individual for whom Jesus died. Let's start loving people in practical ways, and let's teach our children to do the same.

Teaching Younger Preschoolers about People

God designs babies and toddlers to be self-focused for the first two years or so of their lives. As far as they are concerned, the world really does revolve around them. Learning about themselves at this age is foundational to their learning about other people as they mature.

Biblical Concept Statements

- God made me.
- God made me special.
- God created me to make choices.
- God helps me learn.
- God loves for me to talk to Him.
- God helps me grow like Jesus grew.
- God wants me to be a friend.
- God loves me.
- God has plans for me.

- God helps me.
- God helps me learn about Jesus.

Bible-Learning Activities

God created me to make choices.

Our days are filled with choices. As you teach your young pre-schooler that God created him to make choices, provide examples of limited choices. If your child is nonverbal, rather than giving him actual choices you may want to say something like this: "God created you to make choices. We can choose to drink water or milk, eat white cheese or orange cheese, eat apples or bananas, wear green pants or blue pants." Talking about choices with your baby or toddler prepares him for making his own choices as he matures.

God helps me learn and God helps me learn about Jesus.

As you go through your busy day, be sure to plant biblical truth in the mind of your young preschooler. Remind your child that God helps her learn how to eat good food, how to play with toys, how to comb her hair, how to be kind to others, etc. Share with your preschooler that God also helps her learn about Jesus. Look at pictures of Jesus in your child's Bible and say, "We learn about Jesus when we read the Bible." Say a short prayer with your preschooler, thanking God for helping us learn.

God loves for me to talk to Him.

Share with your preschooler that we can talk to God. Model short, simple prayers for your child. Teach your toddler to talk to God by praying, "Thank You, God, for Mommy and Daddy;

thank You, God, for the animals; thank You, God, for good food to eat; thank You, God, for the pretty flowers; thank You, God, for hands to clap and for feet to stomp." Make a habit of talking to God with your younger preschooler in the morning, during the day, and at bedtime.

Teaching Middle Preschoolers about People

There are many things that your middle preschooler needs to understand about God and the people God created in His image. Two- and three-year-olds are beginning to discover they are not the only ones who matter. Find a few minutes throughout the day to teach your child the following biblical truths.

Biblical Concept Statements

- God helps me grow.
- God made me, so I am special.
- God allows me to make right and wrong choices.
- God made me able to think, work, and play.
- God loves for me to pray.
- God helps me grow like Jesus grew.
- God helps me be kind to my friends.
- God will always love me.
- God has a plan for each person.
- God helps me do what He says.
- God wants people to take care of their bodies.
- Jesus taught that I can tell others I'm sorry when I hurt them.
- God wants people to learn from Jesus.

Bible-Learning Activities

God helps me grow and God helps me grow like Jesus grew.

Encourage your child to look in a mirror, preferably a non-breakable hand-held mirror. Say, "God made _____ [insert your preschooler's name in the blank]." While he is still looking in the mirror, softly touch your child on the nose and comment, "God made your nose." Repeat, substituting words such as hair, ears, cheeks, chin, mouth, and eyes. Mention that Jesus also grew. Say, "Your hands are growing just like Jesus' hands grew. Your feet are growing just like Jesus' feet grew. Your hair is growing just like Jesus' hair grew." As your young child grows and develops, he will begin to understand that God made him and helps him grow like Jesus grew.

God wants people to take care of their bodies.

It's never too early to instill this biblical concept in your child's mind. Begin now to help your preschooler develop healthy habits, such as combing her hair, brushing her teeth, washing her hands, taking a bath, and eating good food. Share that God wants us to take care of our bodies. God also wants us to exercise and move our bodies. Encourage outdoor play as often as possible. Allow your child to play in the dirt, pick up sticks, collect rocks, run, and jump.

Teaching Older Preschoolers about People

As your preschooler continues to grow, use the Bible to teach him or her that God has a plan for all people, including your child.

Biblical Concept Statements

- People grow as God planned for them to grow.
- People are special because God made them.
- God allows people to make right and wrong choices.
- God made people able to do many things well.
- God wants people to pray.
- People can try to be like Jesus.
- Jesus taught how God wants us to treat other people.
- No matter what happens, God loves people.
- God has a plan for every person.
- People can show love for God by obeying Him.
- God wants people to take care of their bodies.
- God helps me obey Him.
- Because Jesus forgives, I can tell others I am sorry for hurting them.
- God wants people to follow Jesus' example.

Bible-Learning Activities

People grow as God planned for them to grow.

Start a growth stick. Some people use a door or a wall in a hidden location. Use the growth stick to mark the height of your older preschooler. Kids grow so fast. This will provide a time and location to teach your child that people grow as God planned for them to grow. Show your four- or five-year-old these words in the Bible: "And Jesus increased in wisdom and stature, and in favor with God and with people" (Luke 2:52). Say, "You are growing smarter and stronger like Jesus did. You are also learning about God and how to be kind to your friends like Jesus."

Because Jesus forgives, I can tell others I am sorry for hurting them.

Teaching your preschooler to say, "I'm sorry," is so important. I'm (Ken) not talking about a coerced apology with no real repentance, though. Take advantage of opportunities to teach your child that Jesus forgives us, and Jesus wants us to follow His example. Read Colossians 3:13 to your older preschool: "Just as the Lord has forgiven you, so you are also to forgive." Help your child recognize when and why he needs to say, "I'm sorry."

Teaching Younger Elementary Kids about People

People are everywhere! And, that is a good thing. Help your child know and understand that people are God's most important creation and God helps people make good choices.

Biblical Concept Statements

- Birth and growth are part of God's plan.
- People are God's most important creation.
- God helps people make good choices.
- God wants people to use their talents and abilities in ways that please and honor Him.
- God wants people to pray and read the Bible daily.
- People can follow Jesus' example by obeying God.
- God helps me love others, both friends and enemies.

- Good and bad things happen to people, but God still loves them.
- God has a plan for every person's life.
- God wants people to live every day in ways that please and honor Him.
- People need to take care of their bodies because God created them.
- God helps me obey what is written in the Bible.
- God helps me know when I have hurt others. I can ask them to forgive me.
- God wants our actions, attitudes, thoughts, and words to be good.
- God wants all people to follow Jesus' example.

Bible-Learning Activities

People are God's most important creation.

Gather various craft supplies that you already have in your house such as chenille stems, play dough, construction paper, and washable markers. (It's okay to improvise if you don't have any of those items.) As you read Genesis 1 to your young elementary child, encourage him to make something that God created. Point out that people are God's most important creation. Say, "You are special because God made you. No one else looks, thinks, or acts just like you. And, God has a plan for you. God made everyone special and has a plan for them, too." Pray, thanking God for making your child special.

God helps me love others, both friends and enemies.

Take a few minutes and sit with your child and make a list of their friends. Say, "The Bible tells us, 'A friend loves at all times'" (Prov. 17:17). God gives us friends and helps us love them." Now make a list of your child's enemies. (I pray that list is really short.) Comment that the Bible teaches us to love people who are unkind to us. Jesus said, "Love your enemies, do what is good to those who hate you, bless those who curse you, pray for those who mistreat you" (Luke 6:27–28). Using the two lists, guide your child to pray for his friends *and* his enemies.

God wants our actions, attitudes, thoughts, and words to be good; and God wants all people to follow Jesus' example.

Teaching your child biblical concepts takes place over time while your family goes about its daily routine. As you help your child understand how God wants us to live, take time to define and discuss these terms:

- Actions are the things we do, including how we treat others. Our actions should be loving and kind because Jesus is loving and kind.
- Attitudes are how we feel about something or someone. The Bible says we are to have "the same attitude as that of Christ Jesus" (Phil. 2:5).
- Thoughts are the ideas in our minds. We assume no one knows what we're thinking. However, God knows all our thoughts. The psalmist says, "LORD, you have searched me and known me. You know when I sit down and when I stand up;

you understand my thoughts from far away" (Ps.
139:1–2).
- Words are our thoughts spoken out loud. God
wants all our words to be positive, caring, and
loving. Lead your child to pray this prayer of
King David's: "May the words of my mouth and
the meditation of my heart be acceptable to you,
LORD, my rock and my Redeemer" (Ps. 19:14).

Reinforce the idea that when we follow Jesus' example found
in the Bible, we are living in ways that please God.

Teaching Middle Elementary Kids about People

As your child experiences the middle elementary years, he or
she is seeing more of the difficulties humanity faces. Reassure your
child that even though people may disappoint us, people are still
God's crowning work of creation.

Biblical Concept Statements

- God created me in His image.
- Each person is unique and of value to God.
- People are responsible for their choices.
- People can develop and use their abilities and tal-
ents in ways that please and honor God.
- God wants people to communicate with Him
through praying and reading the Bible daily.
- People can follow the examples, teachings, and
commands of Jesus.
- People can learn to love others as God loves them.

- People can learn to respond in positive ways to what happens to them.
- God wants every person to trust in Jesus as Savior and Lord.
- People can learn about and recognize God's authority.
- People need to take care of their bodies and minds to honor God.
- God asks me to honor Him by choosing to do what is right and rejecting what is wrong.
- The Holy Spirit helps me know that when I have hurt others, I can ask them to forgive me.
- God wants people to have pure thoughts and actions.
- God wants believers to be disciples who grow in their faith and knowledge of Jesus.

Bible-Learning Activities

People can develop and use their abilities and talents in ways that please and honor God.

As you continue to teach your elementary child biblical concepts, remember that family discipleship is an ongoing process. Look for moments throughout the week to share with your child that God wants all of us to use our talents and abilities in ways that please and honor Him. Help your child discover what he does well. Sometimes kids want to play baseball but are unable to stay in the batter's box. Other kids may want to be the next singing sensation but lack the necessary vocal skills. Gently guide your child to recognize his strengths. Allow him to try new skills. Sometimes kids need coaching to develop those skills. Other times they may need to choose something else to do. Read the parable in Matthew 25:14–30 and discuss how your child can use his God-given talents and abilities for God's glory.

People can learn to respond in positive ways to what happens to them.

As we walk through life, we see good and bad things happen to people. Share with your child that God loves people when good things happen, and God loves people when bad things happen. While we can't always control what happens to us, we can choose how we will respond to life's challenges. Summarize and review with your elementary student the life of Joseph in Genesis 37; 39–45. Ask, "If all the bad things Joseph experienced happened to you, how would you respond?" Next, read Genesis 50:15–21. Guide your child to discover Joseph's positive response to the bad things that had happened to him. For further discovery, read 2 Corinthians 11:24–28 and talk about Paul's response to all the difficulties he experienced. Rather than give up, Paul continued to disciple others.

Teaching Preteens about People

Dealing with people can be complicated at times, but when we focus on God's biblical standards for people it becomes much easier. Share the following biblical truths with your preteen to help him or her gain valuable understanding about the people God created.

Biblical Concept Statements

- Life is a gift from God.
- God loves me so I can appreciate my value.
- People are responsible for their choices and any consequences for their actions.
- God will help Christians know and use their spiritual gifts.
- God wants people to communicate with Him and study the Bible daily.
- People can take deliberate actions to grow in Christlikeness.
- People are accountable to God for the way they treat other people.
- People can live with joy regardless of their circumstances.
- God has a plan for each person to understand and follow.
- People can acknowledge and follow God's authority in their lives.
- Because a person's body is God's temple, God wants us to honor Him with our heart, soul, mind, and strength.
- God commands people to obey Him. People can trust that He will help them resist temptation and give them self-control.
- Because of Jesus' death on the cross, we can seek forgiveness from Him and others and restore broken relationships.

- God expects people to remain pure in all aspects of life with their bodies, thoughts, attitudes, actions, and speech.
- God gives each believer one or more spiritual gifts to do His work. God provides resources and other believers to help disciples grow in their faith.

Bible Conversation Starters

People are accountable to God for the way they treat other people.

Take a few minutes to sit with your child and make a list of their friends. Leave some space after each name. Next, ask your preteen to write beside each name what they like and dislike about some of the things that friend does. Read 1 John 3:11–24 and talk about how we can show love to others, even when they do things that irritate us. Mention that God not only helps us love other people, God requires us to love them.

God has a plan for each person to understand and follow.

Spend some time today talking openly with your child about their relationship with Jesus. Share that God wants every person to trust in Jesus as Savior and Lord. If your child has never responded to God's conviction of sin, ask the following questions:

- What do you know about Jesus?
- What is sin?
- What is a cross?
- Why did Jesus have to die on the cross?
- What happened after Jesus died?
- How much does sin cost?

- Who can pay for your sin?
- How do you receive Jesus as Savior and Lord?

Be sensitive to the prompting of the Holy Spirit as you engage in this conversation. If you sense your preteen is not ready to trust in Jesus, don't pressure your child to do so. Come back to the conversation later. For additional guidance, refer to "Appendix A: The Gospel, God's Plan for Me."

Teaching Middle Schoolers about People

Your middle schooler relates to people every day. Offer encouragement as you share the following biblical truths throughout the coming days. Remember, you may have to revisit some of these concepts several times.

Biblical Concept Statements

- All people are created in God's image, and our lives are gifts from God.
- People are created as moral beings and are responsible for their choices, including the ways they treat others.
- Growing in Christlikeness requires our intentional efforts.
- God has a purpose for every person, and He wants us to understand His plans for us.
- God loves all people, regardless of ethnicity or status, and proved His love by sending Jesus to bear the penalty for our sin on the cross.
- Because of Jesus, people can live with joy regardless of circumstances.

- Our response to God's love is to remain pure in all aspects of life, and He empowers us to obey His commands as we live by the Spirit.
- All people have sinned and have been separated from God; but because of Jesus, we can be restored to a relationship with Him.

Bible Conversation Starters

Growing in Christlikeness requires our intentional efforts.

Explore the Gospels—Matthew, Mark, Luke, and John—with your middle schooler and identify words and phrases that describe Jesus' character. Talk about how Jesus, God the Son, obeyed God the Father in how He related to His Father and to people. Mention, "When we follow Jesus' teachings as recorded in the Bible, we are becoming more like Him." Lead your student to think of specific things he can do to "grow in the grace and knowledge of our Lord and Savior Jesus Christ" (2 Pet. 3:18). Be sure to include Bible reading and prayer.

God loves all people, regardless of ethnicity or status, and proved His love by sending Jesus to bear the penalty for our sin on the cross.

Racism is an enormous problem. We often think of racism as a contemporary issue. However, the hatred toward and mistreatment of people based solely on their ethnicity or race has existed since the fall of mankind in the garden of Eden. Ask your middle schooler to name one person that God doesn't love. Follow up your child's response by reading Acts 10:9–48. Ask, "What do you think Peter meant when he said, 'Now I truly understand that God doesn't show favoritism, but in every nation the person who fears him and does what is right is acceptable to him'?" (Acts 10:34–35). God created every person in His image, and He loves everyone. Otherwise, the Bible wouldn't say, "For God loved the world in this way: He gave his one and only Son, so that everyone who believes in him will not perish but have eternal life" (John 3:16).

Teaching High Schoolers about People

The daily life of a high school student is often consumed by relationships with other people. What they wear, what video games they play, what they post on social media, whom they eat lunch with, even where they go to church are often influenced by their peers. Now is not the time to release the walls of parental protection. Guide your high schooler to understand that the boundaries you establish regarding relationships are based on biblical truth and are for their own good.

Biblical Concept Statements

- All people are created in God's image as male and female, are infinitely valuable, and our lives are gifts from God.
- People are created as moral beings and are responsible for their choices and the consequences of their choices, including the ways we treat others.
- We can grow in Christlikeness by acting intentionally to pursue Christ and as God works in our lives.

- God has a purpose for every person, and we can know His plans by understanding and applying the truth of Scripture.
- God loves all people, regardless of ethnicity or status, desires that we would all turn to Him for salvation, and demonstrated His love by sending Jesus to bear the penalty for our sin on the cross.
- Because of Jesus, people can live with joy regardless of circumstances, as joy is rooted in an eternal perspective and not in earthly circumstances.
- Our response to God's love is to remain pure in all aspects of life—with our bodies, thoughts, attitudes, actions, and speech—and He empowers us to obey His commands as we live by the Spirit.
- All people have sinned and have been separated from God; but we can be restored to a relationship with Him when we trust in Jesus and turn from our sin.

Bible Conversation Starters

All people are created in God's image as male and female, are infinitely valuable, and our lives are gifts from God.

Read Genesis 1:26–27 and 2:7, 15–25. Share that all people are created in God's image as male and female. Since we are the only creatures made in God's image, we are the only created beings that can have a personal relationship with the Living God. The Bible also says that God breathed breath into man. We are infinitely valuable because God gives us life. Be prepared to discuss current LGBTQ+ issues. Refrain from becoming angry or defensive if you and your teen disagree on matters related to gender and sexual orientation, including public policy and the theology of manhood and womanhood.

Because of Jesus, people can live with joy regardless of circumstances, as joy is rooted in an eternal perspective and not in earthly circumstances.

So much of a teenager's life is circumstantial—making and losing friends, dating, learning to drive, passing and failing school assignments, winning and losing in sports and the arts, being hired and fired, gaining and losing weight, and so forth. Your high schooler's life often feels like a yo-yo. Encourage your child with the biblical truth that Jesus is "the same yesterday, today, and forever" (Heb. 13:8). Even though an earthly circumstance may feel dire, assure your teen that it is only temporary. Jesus's eternal nature gives us hope that leads to joy. So, let me (Ken) share about some earthly circumstances.

On June 26, 2020, my wife and I received one of those phone calls that as a parent you dread. At about 11:15 p.m. all our phones started ringing. I answered and one of my son's friends was on the phone. He said, "Mr. Hindman, this is _____." He gave his name and identified himself. He said, "There has been an accident with your son in our pool and we have called 911." I said, "Please don't let them leave with my child until I get there."

We got in the car and drove about eight miles. When we turned on the street, all we could see were flashing lights. There were 11 patrol cars, ambulances, and rescue vehicles parked in or near the driveway. Mack was already strapped to a flat board with braces around his neck and upper body. IV drips were in both arms. I shared that I was the father, and the EMT allowed me to step up into the back of the ambulance. Mack was crying from the pain and fear. I prayed over my young adult child that the Lord would watch over him and take care of him as they drove to the hospital. We watched as they left the house, thanked the family for calling, and headed to the hospital.

We arrived at the hospital around 12:30 a.m. And, if you ever wondered what the emergency room of a regional hospital is like on the weekend just take my word, it is something you never want to experience. We were not allowed into the hospital due to COVID-19 rules. We talked with a representative, and they told us they would update us following the triage evaluation. Around 3:00 a.m. we were ushered into the Elvis Presley Conference Room. It was a small room with about eight simple chairs and one piece of artwork with the face of the late Elvis Presley. A young doctor entered the room and asked the following question: "What do you know about the accident your son experienced earlier this evening?" I shared that we got a call that he had been in a diving accident while swimming at a friend's house and that was about all. She then shared with us the news that changed our lives. She said he had shattered his C6 vertebra and is now a quadriplegic, which means he is paralyzed from the chest down.

My heart still breaks when I think about this simple conversation. Our earthly circumstances changed that night. But you know what, nothing about our *eternal* circumstances changed. Yes, this journey is hard. Yes, there are hard days. Yes, there will be many additional hard days ahead. But my joy, our joy as a family, is not rooted in earthly circumstances. Our joy is in the Lord. As His children we can know that "Weeping may stay overnight, but there is joy in the morning" (Ps. 30:5). There is so much more I could share about the earthly journey we are traveling; but let me remind you that because of Jesus, people can live with joy regardless of circumstances, as joy is rooted in an eternal perspective and not in earthly circumstances.

Digging Deeper in Biblical Truth

Use the statements below to help your high schooler think deeply about biblical truth related to people, and to be prepared to defend his beliefs.

Being: Because God created us, we belong to Him, and He has the right to direct our lives for His purposes.

Doing: In order to fulfill God's purposes in our lives, namely reflecting His glory and character, we must know Him personally. Therefore, we should devote ourselves wholeheartedly to living in relationship with Him.

Apologetic: Many today believe that, until a baby is born, he is not a living person. However, Scripture teaches that, from the time we are conceived, all people are living spiritual beings with great worth.

10

Teaching My Family God's Plan for Families

Family. Where does one start when the topic is family? Let me begin by saying that I (Ken) dearly love my family. They are the closest earthly relationships that I have. My wife Kristina and I have been married for twenty-seven years. I am so blessed to be married to Kristina. She is a radiant beauty who loves family and friends deeply. She is the best storyteller I have ever heard. Once you spend time with Kristina, you will be focused on her amazing ability to communicate and share her love for life and the Lord. Her ability to remember details from encounters and experiences is almost unbelievable. Kristina is the heartbeat of our home and family.

We are blessed with two boys who are now young men. Mack (twenty-one) is a college student and has surrendered his life to the Lord for full-time Christian ministry. Mack is dearly loved by many. He has impressive abilities for communication and relating to others. He just makes you feel comfortable. David (nineteen) is a college freshman and loves to debate. David is still seeking the Lord for His plan for David's life. He loves to be surrounded by

people and leads others well. We are so thankful for the blessing
of family.

Read the Bible

As a family we still make eating together throughout the week
a priority. We all love to eat. We also enjoy opening our home to
guests and are thankful for the resources the Lord has provided
that He uses for His glory through our family. Kristina and I have
always made it a priority to be engaged with our kids. Not just
every once in a while, but all the time. We were there watching,
listening, supporting, and encouraging. Music, sports, education,
church, movies, and birthday parties, we were there. Why? That's
what God had called us to do.

Being present in our sons' lives allowed us to continue teaching biblical truth and to disciple them through the challenges they
faced growing up. Family is not easy. If it were, I'm not sure Paul
would have written, "Children, obey your parents in the Lord,
because this is right. Honor your father and mother, which is the
first commandment with a promise, so that it may go well with you
and that you may have a long life in the land. Fathers, don't stir
up anger in your children, but bring them up in the training and
instruction of the Lord" (Eph. 6:1–4).

Think about the Bible

The Bible has a lot to say about families. And, many of those
Bible families were messy. Even the seemingly ideal families had
problems. Abel's brother killed him, Jacob's brother wanted to
kill him, Joseph's brothers sold him, and Moses' brother betrayed

him. Nevertheless, God chose the image of family to illustrate His relationship with the New Testament church. Family is important, and God created your family for His glory and His purpose. So, remain steadfast and fight for your family.

Teaching Younger Preschoolers about Family

As you share with your younger preschooler about family, do so with love, care, and a tender heart. Your baby and younger preschooler listens to you and begins to develop emotions based on the sounds of your voice. As you teach biblical truths related to the family, use a calm tender voice.

Biblical Concept Statements

- God made families.
- Families love one another.
- God gave me a mommy and daddy to help me.
- My family tells me about God.
- God loves families.

Bible-Learning Activities

God made families and God loves families.

Teaching your younger preschooler that God made his/her family should be fun. I suggest using a family picture. Show the picture to your younger preschooler and share that God made families. Practice this simple activity with some method of consistency when you diaper your child, feed your child in the highchair, and rock your child to sleep. This will help your baby or toddler begin to identify her family. When she touches and holds the picture, remind your young preschooler that the Bible tells us God made families. Point to each family member and say, "God loves _____ [insert family member's name]."

My family tells me about God.

If your baby or toddler were verbal, would he be able to make this claim truthfully? Telling your preschooler about God is as simple as going on a walk and saying, "God made the flowers. Thank You, God, for eyes to see the pretty yellow flowers." I encourage you to spend time daily sharing valuable biblical truths with your child. I suggest you use an open Bible as you share about God. This will help your preschooler begin to recognize that God is real.

Teaching Middle Preschoolers about Family

Where would we be without family? God designed the family to bring Him honor and glory. Teaching your middle preschooler about family is a daily process. Here are a few suggestions to help:

Biblical Concept Statements

- God's plan for families is in the Bible.
- God wants family members to love and help one another.
- God's plan is for children to do what their parents tell them to do.
- Families talk to God and read the Bible.
- God loves families even when bad things happen.

Bible-Learning Activities

God wants family members to love and help one another.

Provide opportunities for your middle preschooler to help you with simple tasks, such as feeding the family pet, watering potted plants, putting clothes in the dyer, and picking up toys. Comment, "The Bible teaches family members to love and help one another. You are doing what the Bible says when you help pick up your toys."

Families talk to God and read the Bible.

When you prepare to pray with your preschooler, share that your family talks to God. Establish family traditions such as praying before every meal. You may choose to hold hands around the table, or your family may prefer to pray with folded hands. Mention that your family also reads the Bible together to learn about God. Here are a few choices that will provide excellent listening sessions for your preschooler: Genesis 1; Exodus 2:1–10; Luke 2:1–7; Luke 2:41–52; and John 1:1–5.

Teaching Older Preschoolers about Family

Families come in all shapes and sizes. Are you a single parent raising your four- or five-year-old? You are a family. Are you a grandparent who is the primary caregiver for your preschool grandchild? You are a family. Are you a mom and dad with six kids all under the age of ten? You are a family.

Biblical Concept Statements

- God's plan for families is for mothers and fathers to raise children. Children are born or adopted into families.
- God wants families to show love, respect, and kindness to one another.
- God's plan is for children to obey their parents.
- Families worship God together.
- When two people marry, they become a family. Adam and Eve were the first family.
- God loves families even when they hurt each other, and He wants families to forgive each other.

Bible-Learning Activities

God wants families to show love, respect, and kindness to one another.

Do you raise your voice when you are frustrated? I challenge you to talk as a family and make a new rule that no one in the family can raise his or her voice when angry. Set a goal such as, "No one can yell or scream out of frustration for the next _____ [fill in the blank with one day, three days, or five days]." This little experiment will demonstrate to your older preschooler love, respect, and kindness.

When two people marry, they become a family. Adam and Eve were the first family.

With your preschooler, look at photographs taken at your wedding. Explain that when two people get married, they become a family. Open your Bible to Genesis 2 and talk about Adam and

Eve who were the first family. Share that mommy and daddy love each other and love the family that God created on the day you were married. To make this conversation more memorable, consider eating cake together and pretending it's a wedding cake.

Teaching Younger Elementary Kids about Family

As your child expands his social circle, he or she most likely will be exposed to families that are quite different from your family. Some of these other families may even practice lifestyles contrary to what is biblical. Teach your young elementary child the standards God gives families, while also teaching your child that God loves everyone.

Biblical Concept Statements

- God's plan for mothers and fathers is to be examples of God's love.
- God's plan for families is for them to love, respect, and help one another.
- God tells children to respect and obey their parents.
- God wants families to worship at home and other places.
- In a marriage, a man and a woman make promises to God and each other.
- God loves families and wants families to love and forgive each other when difficult things happen.

Bible-Learning Activities

God wants families to worship at home and other places.

Talk with your child about worship. Mention that worship is our response to God's love for us. We can worship anytime and anywhere. Share that when your child prays and reads his Bible, he or she is worshiping God. Talk about ways your family can worship together, including different places where worship can take place. Plan a family worship experience with your child. Include elements such as prayer, singing, and Bible reading. Assign one family member to pray, one to lead the family to sing, and another to read the Bible.

God loves families and wants families to love and forgive each other when difficult things happen.

Gather a sheet of paper and a pen or pencil. Divide the paper into two columns. At the top of one column, write the word, *Happy*. Write, *Sad*, at the top of the other column. Guide your child to list in the appropriate column family experiences that make them happy or sad. Share with your child that God loves your family even when bad things happen, and God wants family members to love and forgive each other. Look at your child's two lists and encourage your six- or seven-year-old to forgive a family member who has upset them. Lead your child to pray for your family.

Teaching Middle Elementary Kids about Family

Your eight- or nine-year old is growing up in a world in which the idea of family has become convoluted in order to fit the social norms of the day. Use the following biblical concepts and Bible-learning activities to help your child understand God's standard for families.

Biblical Concept Statements

- God's plan for mothers and fathers is to teach their children about God. Parents are examples of how God is our heavenly Father.
- God's plan is for all family members to work together so that God is honored by their family.
- God expects children to honor Him in the way they honor their parents.
- God wants families to worship together to help them grow stronger in their faith.
- In a wedding ceremony, a man and a woman make promises to God, to each other, and to all those present to be committed to each other through good and bad times.
- God loves families even when family members sin. God is always ready to forgive.

Bible-Learning Activities

God's plan for mothers and fathers is to teach their children about God. Parents are examples of how God is our heavenly Father.

At first glance, this biblical concept may seem directed more toward you as a parent than to your kids. However, teaching your child about God's plan for mothers and fathers is critical. Help your elementary student find and read Deuteronomy 6:4–9. Guide your child to list parents' responsibilities found in this passage. Next, ask, "Even though Moses is speaking primarily to adults, what do you think your responsibility as a kid is?" Share that God wants every member of the family to love God and live in ways that honor Him. Continue the conversation by talking about how God is our Father. If your child has an absentee father, reassure your kid that as our heavenly Father God will always be with him or her.

God's plan is for all family members to work together so that God is honored by their family.

What are you doing as a family to work together? Ask your child for three suggestions of how the entire family can work together. Cleaning the house, working in the yard, folding the laundry, and washing the car are all ways you can please God with how you work as a family. If you go outside to work, guide your child to look at the ants scurrying across the ground. Ask if your child has ever seen an ant remain still. Mention that the Bible says, "Go to the ant, you slacker! Observe its ways and become wise. Without leader, administrator, or ruler, it prepares its provisions in summer; it gathers its food during harvest" (Prov. 6:6–8).

Teaching Preteens about Family

During this awkward stage between childhood and adolescence, your preteen is flexing those independent muscles. Your almost-teenager will enjoy spending time together as a family. However, no matter how wonderful your family is, as soon as your preteen's friends appear, she'll act like you're some kind of alien from outer space. Hang in there! You are still the parent. This too shall pass.

Biblical Concept Statements

- Families are a part of God's plan for providing for children's spiritual, physical, mental, social, and emotional needs.
- God's plan is for each person to make a positive contribution to her family. Men and women have different but complementary roles in the family.
- God expects children to honor Him in the ways they honor their parents throughout their lives.
- God wants families to have an attitude of worship.
- A man and a woman marry in a covenant relationship, promising to love each other until death as God loves them.
- God loves families even when they are broken. God wants all believers to act as the family of God and help others in difficult times.

Bible Conversation Starters

A man and a woman marry in a covenant relationship, promising to love each other until death as God loves them.

You may have had a similar conversation about marriage when your preteen was a preschooler or elementary student. Perhaps now is the time to take the next step by addressing biblical marriage in light of what your preteen is hearing about the LBGTQ+ community. Read Genesis 2:21–25 and Mark 10:2–9. Explain that when two people get married, a man and woman make a promise to God and each other—in the presence of witnesses—to be committed to each other through good and bad times. That promise is to love each other until death, "just as Christ loved the church and gave himself for her" (Eph. 5:25). If divorce is a reality in your family, assure your preteen that God still loves you, your child, and your family.

God loves families even when they are broken. God wants all believers to act as the family of God and help others in difficult times.

Ask your almost-teenager to define *family*. Take the time with your preteen to talk about families in general. Ask, "What people are in your friends' families?" Next, talk about ways your family is the same and different from other families. Your preteen probably knows a family that is going through difficulty. Share with your child that God loves families even when they are broken. Comment that even your family seems broken at times. Mention that God loves your family, and He wants families to forgive each other when difficult things happen. Read James 1:27 and share that God wants all believers to act as the family of God and help others in difficult times. List ways your family can help other families and spend time praying for your friends' broken families.

Teaching Middle Schoolers about Family

Middle schoolers are impacted by a variety of different families each and every day. I encourage you to make sure that your middle schooler has an understanding of God's plan for the family so your young teenager can navigate the unique conversations they may encounter with friends.

Biblical Concept Statements

- Families are part of God's plan for filling the earth with His image-bearers and His glory and are responsible for providing for the needs of family members.
- God's plan for the family involves one man and one woman, committing to one another in a life-long covenant relationship as a reflection of God's love for His people.
- God calls children to honor their parents throughout their lives as a reflection of their honor and love for Him.
- When families experience brokenness, God desires to bring healing and unity and to use the broader family of God to minister to hurting families during difficult times.

Bible Conversation Starters

Families are part of God's plan for filling the earth with His image-bearers and His glory and are responsible for providing for the needs of family members.

Teaching your child about God's plan for families will equip your middle schooler to defend his beliefs when others accuse him of holding onto an antiquated family model. Ask, "Why do you think God instructed Adam and Eve to 'Be fruitful, multiply, fill the earth' (Gen. 1:28)? Why did God repeat this command after the flood when he told Noah to 'be fruitful and multiply; spread out over the earth and multiply on it'" (Gen. 9:7)? Continue the conversation by asking what an *image-bearer* is (see 1 Cor.

15:47–49). Ask, "How does bearing the image of Christ propel us to help provide for the needs of other family members?" Pray with your middle schooler, asking God to help your family reflect God's glory to a broken and sinful world.

God calls children to honor their parents throughout their lives as a reflection of their honor and love for Him.

God calls each of your children to obey you. Ask, "What is 'the first commandment with a promise'" (Eph. 6:2)? Lead in a discussion of what honoring Mom and Dad should look like in your family. Read Colossians 3:20 and share that a love for God gives kids the desire to honor their parents through obedience, "for this pleases the Lord" (Col. 3:20).

Teaching High Schoolers about Family

Your high schooler needs your wisdom and guidance from a biblical perspective related to families. They see and experience many different family structures in life, but your advice and teaching can keep them pointed in the right direction that honors God and His Word.

Biblical Concept Statements

- Families are a part of God's plan for filling the earth with His image-bearers and are responsible for providing for the spiritual, physical, mental, social, and emotional needs of family members.
- God's plan for the family involves one man and one woman, who have different but complementary roles, committing to one another in a lifelong

covenant relationship as a reflection of God's love for His people.

- God calls children to honor their parents throughout their lives as a reflection of honor and love for Him. Further, we are to demonstrate love toward all members of our families, including siblings, extended family, and those whom God brings into our families as a result of fostering, adoption, or remarriage.
- When families experience brokenness, such as conflict, abuse, or divorce, God desires to bring healing and unity and to use the broader family of God to minister to hurting families during difficult times.

Bible Conversation Starters

Families are a part of God's plan for filling the earth with His image-bearers and are responsible for providing for the spiritual, physical, mental, social, and emotional needs of family members.

Open this conversation by reading Luke 2:41–52. Ask your high schooler what parts of this Bible story resonate with him or her the most. Ask, "What does this passage say about the relationship between kids and parents? What are the parents' and kids' responsibilities?" Focus on verse 52: "And Jesus increased in wisdom and stature, and in favor with God and with people" (Luke 2:52). Mention that Jesus had some of the same needs we have today. Lead a discussion about how parents, teens, and younger siblings can provide for one another's spiritual, physical, mental, social, and emotional needs.

God's plan for the family involves one man and one woman, who have different but complementary roles, committing to one another in a lifelong covenant relationship as a reflection of God's love for His people.

Read Ephesians 5:22–33 and talk about the roles of husbands and wives in the family. Note the parallels Paul makes between a married couple and the church. Ask, "Why do you think Paul uses marriage as an illustration of the church?" Allow for an open discussion and respond to your high schooler's comments and questions lovingly and honestly. If your teenage daughter bristles at the phrase, "Submit to your husbands," or your teenage son flexes his muscles at the words, "The husband is the head of the wife" (Eph. 5:22–23), point out that the picture here is of the relationship between Jesus and His bride the church. Explain that both men and women are created in God's image and have equal worth and value before God the Father. Furthermore, men and women have different but complementary roles in the family. The bottom line is that in a biblical marriage, husbands and wives respect and honor each other as an outflow of their love for Christ Jesus.

Digging Deeper in Biblical Truth

Use the statements below to help your high schooler think deeply about God's design for family and to be prepared to defend his beliefs.

Being: Because we were meant to live in relationship, God's design is that we would experience love, acceptance, support, and guidance through an earthly family. Further, God's children are part of a spiritual family, the church, where we experience these, and we find all of these perfectly in God, our Father.

Doing: We are called to honor God in the ways we treat our family. Therefore, we should work to intentionally show family members love and forgiveness.

Apologetic: Many people today believe the definition of marriage is subjective and flexible, and that as long as people "love" each other, they have the right to be "married." However, the Bible clearly defines marriage as a covenant relationship between one man and one woman for life.

11

Teaching My Family How to Relate to the Community and World

Take a moment and think about the community where you live. Do you know your neighbors? What about the person across the street? What does your community need from you and your family? In the next few pages, we will take a closer look at God's plan for the community and world where we live.

Read the Bible

God has a plan for your neighborhood, community, town, city, state, region, country, and the entire world. As Jesus prepared to physically leave His disciples for the final time, He said, "But you will receive power when the Holy Spirit has come on you, and you will be my witnesses in Jerusalem, in all Judea and Samaria, and to the ends of the earth" (Acts 1:8). Notice that Jesus didn't ask if His disciples *wanted* to spread the gospel. Jesus told them that they *would* proclaim the good news about Him.

Think about the Bible

God has a plan for all communities and for people all over the world. What is that plan? What can you do? Sometimes, I (Ken) think we are more worried about locking our doors, closing our windows, building fences, and keeping people out rather than letting them in. Yes, I watch the news. Yes, I see the issues we have. But, I am reminded that God has not been surprised by one thing. He is still God. He is still on the throne, and God is still in control. Almighty God is calling us to leave our fear behind and impact those around us. Are you ready for that? I pray you are, and more importantly, I pray that you disciple your preschooler, elementary child, preteen, or teenager to be ready to change the world for the glory of the Lord.

Teaching Younger Preschoolers about the Community and World

The world of your young preschooler naturally revolves around him or her. Part of your job as a parent is to help your child begin to recognize that he or she is not the center of the universe. Use the biblical concept statements and Bible-learning activities below to help your baby or toddler discover that God loves her and God loves other people, too.

Biblical Concept Statements

- God made people.
- God helps people.
- People tell about God and Jesus.

- People can talk with God.
- God cares about other people and me.

Bible-Learning Activities

God helps people.

Helping others is a life lesson all of us need to learn. Teach your younger preschooler that God helps people. As you help your toddler work a puzzle, say, "God helps people. Daddy is helping you put the puzzle together." Remember that these early years are a time of building foundations. Even though babies and young toddlers don't understand fully the concept of helping, you can lay the groundwork for future learning by repeating the Bible phrase, "God helps me" (Heb. 13:6).

God cares about other people and me.

Whenever your baby or toddler needs to be comforted, softly say the Bible phrase, "God cares for you" (1 Pet. 5:7). Share with your young preschooler a few examples of how God demonstrates His care for your child and family. Comment that God cares about how we feel, how we grow, and how we learn.

Teaching Middle Preschoolers about the Community and World

What do you see when you drive through the streets of your neighborhood, community, and city? How are you, as a parent, teaching your preschooler about the community and world in which we live? Here are a few simple suggestions that will help lay a foundation for your child to begin to understand how he or she can relate to others in our community and in our world.

Biblical Concept Statements

- God made people alike and different.
- God helps all people.
- People tell others about God and Jesus.
- People can pray for others.
- People are important to God.
- Missionaries are people who tell other people about God and Jesus.

Bible-Learning Activities

God made people alike and different.

Provide baby dolls for your preschooler that represent races and ethnicities other than your own. Do the same for toy people figures. As your young child plays with the dolls and people figures, he may voice his observations related to the differences in skin tone or other physical characteristics. If he does, take the opportunity to celebrate the ways people are alike and different. Comment, "The Bible tells us that 'God made us' (Ps. 100:3), and 'God loves us'" (1 John 4:10).

People tell other people about God and Jesus.

Gather a toy phone or an old mobile phone. As an option collect an old computer keyboard and a small box, or a clean pizza box and a keyboard. Decorate the tall side of the small box or the inside lid of the pizza box to look like a computer monitor. Place the keyboard in front of the small box, or inside the bottom of the pizza carton. Encourage your preschooler to tell someone about God and Jesus on the "phone" and/or "computer." You might be thinking, *Why should I teach my preschooler about telling others about God and Jesus? My child can barely speak plainly.* Simply put, if you teach your two- or three-year-old the importance of sharing Jesus at this age, they grow up thinking that telling others about God and Jesus is a natural thing to do.

Teaching Older Preschoolers about the Community and World

Does your four- or five-year-old participate in a part-time or full-time day care, preschool program, or homeschool co-op? If so, she is learning how God made people alike and different. Consider using the following biblical truths and suggested activities to help your preschooler learn how God wants us to relate to people in our community and world.

Biblical Concept Statements

- God made people alike and different, and all are special to Him.
- God helps people do His work.
- People who love God tell others all over the world about Him.
- People can pray for others in their communities and world.
- The Bible tells me to love others in my community and world.
- Missionaries tell people about God and Jesus in my country and in other countries.

Bible-Learning Activities

God made people alike and different, and all are special to Him.

Compile online photographs of people of various nationalities, races, ethnicities, ages, body types, and special needs. As you look at the pictures with your preschooler, state, "We all look different, and God made and loves all of us." List differences among family members, such as Mommy is pretty and Daddy is handsome, Brother is short and Sister is tall, Grams has gray hair and Granddaddy has none. Keep the comments positive to help your child understand that everyone is special to God.

Missionaries tell people about God and Jesus in my country and in other countries.

Does your preschooler understand the work that a missionary does? Explain that missionaries are people—men, women, and families—who tell other people about God and Jesus. Share that missionaries live all over the world. Using an inflatable globe or a printed world map, play a find-the-missionary game. Allow your preschooler to point to a place on the globe or map and say, "Missionaries can tell the people in _____ [insert name of the country or state] about Jesus." Continue playing as long as your child shows interest. Pray, asking God to help missionaries tell people around the world about Jesus.

Teaching Younger Elementary Kids about the Community and World

The older your child becomes the more he or she will notice that people look, act, and talk differently. Using the following concept statements and activities, lead your elementary student to understand that God loves and values everyone.

Biblical Concept Statements

- God values all people.
- God helps people to do His work in their communities and world.
- Christians are called to tell people all over the world about Jesus.
- People can pray for people all over the world.
- The Bible tells me to love others in my community and world.
- Missionaries are called by God to tell another group of people the good news about Jesus.

Bible-Learning Activities

God helps people to do His work in their communities and world.

Does your church do ministry in your community and world, such as take meals to people who can't cook or leave their homes? Collect backpacks filled with food for school kids whose families don't have enough food to eat on the weekends? Collect warm clothes for people who are homeless? Host block parties? Conduct Vacation Bible School in the city park? Send people on mission trips to other states or countries? Churches that follow Jesus' directive in Acts 1:8 do those kinds of things, and your young elementary child can help. Ministry is not a task just for adults. Find ways to involve your family in the work God is doing in your community, city, state, nation, and world.

Christians are called to tell people all over the world about Jesus.

Does your elementary child observe your telling people about Jesus? Read Matthew 28:18–20 and ask your child to whom Jesus' words apply. Point out that Jesus expects His followers to tell people in all nations about Him. Ask your pastor for the names of a missionary family that your family could "adopt." As a family correspond with that missionary family, exchange family pictures, send them care packages, and pray regularly for them. Who knows? One day your elementary student may be a missionary in another country because of how God is working through your family now.

Teaching Middle Elementary Kids about the Community and World

Eight- and nine-year-olds can sometimes be mean to people who are different from them. Your child might be the target of that unfortunate behavior, or your elementary student may be one of the culprits. Teaching your child the following biblical concepts is critical to his or her spiritual growth.

Biblical Concept Statements

- Even before they are born, people are special to God.

- God works through people to do work in their communities and world.
- All Christians are called to be on mission with God.
- People can pray for specific needs of others.
- God tells me to connect with others and show them His love.
- Missionaries are Christians called by God to tell another group of people the good news about Jesus.

Bible-Learning Activities

Even before they are born, people are special to God.

When my (Landry's) two sons were in elementary school, our neighbor's kids informed them that a certain fast-food chain killed babies. That opened up a conversation my wife and I weren't ready to have. Fortunately, we had been teaching our two boys that everyone is special to God. Read Jeremiah 1:5 and Psalm 139:13–16 with your child. Say, "God knew you before you were born, because God created you." Ask, "How does that make you feel? How does this truth impact your attitude toward others?" If appropriate, pray, asking for forgiveness for not valuing people as God's special creation.

People can pray for specific needs of others.

I (Landry) remember attending Bible study one evening when the all-too-familiar sound of sirens pierced the chapel walls. The pastor paused from teaching and recalled that he knew of another pastor who said that whenever he heard sirens, he would immediately pray for the first responders and for any potential victims. That was more than twenty-five years ago, and I still keep that practice. People next door and across the globe are hurting. Teach your child to pray for people he knows, as well as for people he doesn't know. Encourage your elementary student to start a prayer journal and to begin listing and praying for specific needs of other people.

Teaching Preteens about the Community and World

Please realize the importance of helping your preteen understand that the community and world around him or her needs to know about Jesus. Guide your almost-teenager to acknowledge that God values people everywhere.

Biblical Concept Statements

- God values all people everywhere, both unborn and born, from every race, ethnicity, and culture.
- God allows people to join Him in His work throughout the world.
- God calls all Christians to tell people about Jesus and to teach them how to know and follow God.
- People can pray for missionaries and the people they teach and serve.
- God tells me to connect with all types of people and show them His love.
- Missionaries are Christians called by God to boldly tell another group of people the good news about Jesus, no matter the danger.

Bible Conversation Starters

God values all people everywhere, both unborn and born, from every race, ethnicity, and culture.

The genocide taking place in other nations is heartbreaking. So is the deliberate abortion of unborn babies. Regretfully, your preteen most likely already knows about both. If you haven't talked with your almost-teenager about the killing of unborn children and the slaughter of people based on their ethnicity, consider approaching the subject with sensitivity and compassion. Read Psalm 139 together and discuss the value God places on all human life, from conception to death.

God tells me to connect with all types of people and show them His love.

John 3:16 has been made popular by Christian athletes and their fans, and your preteen is probably familiar with this important Bible verse. However, your preteen needs to know more context of the verse. Read John 3:1–21 and talk about Jesus' earthly mission. Focus on verses 17–18 and the implication that our sharing God's love with others is imperative.

Teaching Middle Schoolers about the Community and World

Your middle schooler will enjoy exploring this topic because your child lives in a world that is impacted by an aggressively changing culture. Helping your young teen navigate the community and world based on biblical truth will be a great benefit throughout the coming years.

Biblical Concept Statements

- God values all people and calls Christians to live on mission for the sake of reaching the lost with the gospel.
- God continues to work in the world, and people are invited to join Him in His work.
- We are to be involved in reaching the nations through prayer, giving resources, loving actions, and sharing the gospel.

Bible Conversation Starters

God values all people and calls Christians to live on mission for the sake of reaching the lost with the gospel.

Invite your middle schooler to read 1 John 4:19–21. Ask your teen about the meaning of this verse: "We love because he first loved us" (1 John 4:19–21). Share with your middle schooler that the Bible teaches that our motivation to love people in our community and world is the love God has for each of us. That same love compels us to make sharing the gospel part of our everyday lives.

We are to be involved in reaching the nations through prayer, giving resources, acting with love, and sharing the gospel.

Does your middle schooler understand what a missionary does? The dangers missionaries encounter day after day? Remind your teenager that missionaries are people just like us whom God has called to take the gospel to the nations. Share that missionaries live all over the world, some in parts of the world so dangerous that the missionaries cannot disclose their actual location. Talk about ways your family can help reach the nations. Praying and giving money are both an obvious and essential response. There's more that your young teen can do, though. The world is coming to us. Coach your middle schooler so he will be ready to share about his faith in Jesus with classmates and neighbors from other nations.[1]

Teaching High Schoolers about the Community and World

How can your high school student impact the community and world where he or she lives? Only the Lord knows the answer to that question. I (Ken) am asking you to do your part to prepare your high schooler for that task. The following statements and discussion suggestions are a starting point for that preparation.

Biblical Concept Statements

- God values all people—born and unborn, young and old, male and female, all ethnicities, those of opposing faiths—and calls Christians to live on mission for the sake of reaching the lost across the street and around the world through prayer, giving resources, acting with love, and sharing the gospel.
- God continues to work in the world, and as we join Him in His work, He uses people to accomplish His eternal purposes.
- We demonstrate honor for God when we respect the earthly authorities God has placed in our lives, including parents, pastors, teachers, coaches, police, and government.

Bible Conversation Starters

God values all people—born and unborn, young and old, male and female, all ethnicities, those of opposing faiths— and calls Christians to live on mission for the sake of reaching the lost across the street and around the world through prayer, giving resources, acting with love, and sharing the gospel.

A lot of truth is packed in this biblical concept. Let's start with the value God places on each individual. Tackle difficult sanctity of life issues including abortion, euthanasia, and the death penalty. As your high schooler grapples with these issues, point him to Bible verses such as Exodus 20:13; Matthew 5:21–22; and Romans 13:9. Congruent to these issues, is God's love for all people. Read Revelation 5:8–10 and point out that Jesus died for everyone in every nation. The gospel is not bound by geopolitical boundaries or ethnic and racial differences.

We demonstrate honor for God when we respect the earthly authorities God has placed in our lives, including parents, pastors, teachers, coaches, police, and government.

Adherence to this biblical concept is desperately needed in today's society. Read 1 Peter 2:13–17. Engage your high schooler in a conversation about the correlation between honoring God and respecting earthly authority. Lead your student to understand that we are required by the authority of God to respect and follow the authorities placed in our lives. You will know your child is following the Bible's teachings about authority when your student obeys her parents; listens to the points of the pastor's weekly message;

follows the directions given by classroom teachers; learns from the coach's instructions; pulls over when the lights of the police car appear in the rearview mirror; and abides by local, state, and federal laws.

Digging Deeper in Biblical Truth

Use the statements below to help your high schooler think deeply about his community and world, and to be prepared to defend his beliefs.

Being: As God's people, we are ambassadors called to reach the world with the gospel.

Doing: As God's representatives, we should devote our lives to loving all people well and reaching them with the gospel that they could be reconciled to God.

Apologetic: Many people today believe the universe exists as the result of some great cosmic accident and that people evolved from simpler life forms. However, the Bible teaches that our loving Father created us to live in relationship with Him and to reflect His glory to others. Therefore, every person possesses inherent dignity and worth.

12

Teaching My Family
about the Church

I (Ken) love the local church. All my life, the Lord has allowed
me to worship, attend, and serve some amazing churches. These
churches have been the sources of enthusiastic worship, in-depth
Bible study, relationships, encouragement, comfort, spiritual and
physical food, programs, missions, giving, rest and leadership
development, training, and many other blessings; but what is most
important to me is the way the church teaches me how to serve
others.

Read the Bible

Acts 2:41–47 paints a wonderful picture of the church. As
you read the passage, underline or jot down characteristics of the
early church. The local church has many functions, and all are
important and serve a purpose. As your child ages, he or she may
question why church is important. The writer of Hebrews tells us
to "watch out for one another to provoke love and good works, not

neglecting to gather together, as some are in the habit of doing, but encouraging each other" (Heb. 10:24–25).

Think about the Bible

Lest you think the early church was the epitome of Christian unity, read some of what Paul wrote to churches in his thirteen letters. Paul both commended and chastised his fellow believers. Churches today would do well to heed Paul's words. As you prepare to teach your kids about the church, think through some of these questions: What is the biblical purpose of the local church? Do all local churches follow the biblical standard? Should churches teach people to serve, lead, or both? What should I do when I attend a local church?

Ask yourself these additional questions: Does the local church I attend teach the Bible from Genesis to Revelation? Support missions all over the world? Preach a message of evangelism? Teach age-suitable biblical truth for preschoolers through senior adults? Offer help for the needs represented in my community, city, and state? Make decisions autonomously, or follow the dictates of a centralized authority? Believe the Bible, teach the Bible, and live by the truths of the Bible?

You may not be able answer all those questions; however, you still have a responsibility to lead your family spiritually. The following pages provide guidance as you lead your preschooler, elementary child, preteen, middle schooler, and high school student to understand God's purpose for His church.

Teaching Younger Preschoolers about the Church

How will you teach your child that people at church love them and are there to help them? The following biblical concepts and activity suggestions provide an excellent starting point for you and your family.

Biblical Concept Statements

- People learn about God and Jesus at church.
- People at church love me.
- People at church help me.
- People at church sing, talk to God, and listen to Bible stories.

Bible-Learning Activities

People at church love me.

When I (Ken) grew up, my parents would begin preparing our family for Sunday morning church on Saturday afternoon. They talked about the activities I enjoyed most at church, the people at church I would see, and how much the preschool volunteers loved me. We even laid out all our clothes for Sunday. When do you prepare for church? If you wait until Sunday morning, you might want to consider an earlier start. As you get ready, remind your younger preschooler that people at church love him.

People at church sing, talk to God, and listen to Bible stories.

Open your Bible to Luke 2. Share with your preschooler that people at church sing, pray (talk to God), and learn from the Bible. Tell your young child the story about Jesus' birth from Luke 2:1–7.

Next, sing a favorite Christmas song about Jesus. Comment that the Bible story and the song are both about Jesus being born. Pray a simple prayer with your child such as, "Thank You, God, for sending Jesus to be born in a manger."

Teaching Middle Preschoolers about the Church

Do you love going to church? Your middle preschooler will begin to develop her beliefs about church and her love for church as she watches you. Set a positive example by prioritizing weekly church attendance for your family.

Biblical Concept Statements

- People use the Bible to learn about God and Jesus at church.
- People at church love each other and teach about God and Jesus.
- People at church help others.
- People at church worship by singing, talking to God, and listening to Bible stories.
- People give money at church.
- Jesus had a special meal with His friends.
- The Bible has stories about baptism.

Bible-Learning Activities

People use the Bible to learn about God and Jesus at church.

I (Ken) am fortunate to serve a church where two- and three-year-olds are taught the Bible every time they are at church. We encourage parents to partner with us in the task of teaching their preschooler about God and Jesus from the Bible. One way in which you can partner with your church's preschool ministry is to ask your preschooler to tell you about the Bible story she learned. Asking if your child had fun is the easy, go-to question often heard in the preschool hall at church. While we want our kids to have fun at church, our desire is for that fun to be secondary to learning from the Bible. Continue the Bible teaching at home by completing the activities on your child's take-home page.

People give money at church.

Tell your preschooler the Bible story from Luke 21:1–4. If you are able to locate a picture of the story, show it to your child. Talk about the people who gave money at the temple (church). Point out that the woman gave all the money she had. Talk about why people give money at your church and what that money is used for. Ask if your preschooler would like to start giving money at church. My mom and dad taught me the importance of giving money at church. I remember as a preschooler placing a quarter in a small basket in my Sunday School class. When I grew older, the quarter increased from one quarter to two quarters each week! In second grade, I started giving my weekly offering in a pre-printed envelope that I would place in the offering plate during the worship service. I grew up thinking everyone gave an offering at church. But that's not the case, is it? However, you can start now building a strong foundation of faithful giving in the life of your preschooler.

Teaching Older Preschoolers about the Church

Older preschoolers still view church as a place where they learn, have fun, and play with friends. Use the foundational concepts below to help your child begin to associate the idea of church more with the people of the church and less with a physical location.

Biblical Concept Statements

- The church is people who gather to learn about God and Jesus from the Bible.
- Church helpers teach about God and Jesus.
- The church provides ways for people to help others.
- People at church worship by praying, giving, singing, reading the Bible, and learning more about God and Jesus.
- People give money at church to help others learn about God and Jesus.
- The Lord's Supper is a special meal to remember Jesus.
- A person is baptized after he or she becomes a Christian.

Bible-Learning Activities

The church is people who gather to learn about God and Jesus from the Bible, and church helpers teach about God and Jesus.

Perhaps you recall from your childhood this simple fingerplay: "Here's the church/Here's the steeple/Open the door/And see all the people!" Consider locating a demonstration online and teaching your older preschooler this fun rhyme. Talk about the people with your child. Share, "Mr. _____ and Mrs. _____ teach you Bible stories. Pastor _____ also tells us about God and Jesus." Pray, thanking God for your church's pastors, teachers, and helpers.

The church provides ways for people to help others.

The next time you arrive at your church, help your child count the number of people who help you and your older preschooler—parking lot volunteers, door greeters, check-in volunteers, classroom teachers, etc. Each of these men and women are there to help you and your preschooler. Inform the church helpers your four- or five-year-old is learning that people at church help others. Share with your child how the people at church are there to help in many ways. Ask your preschooler how she can help others at church.

Teaching Younger Elementary Kids about the Church

Does your six- or seven-year-old enjoy going to church? Why or why not? Model for your child regular church attendance and a healthy attitude toward church.

Biblical Concept Statements

- The church is more than a building; it is Christians who gather to worship and serve God.
- Church leaders are chosen to teach about God and Jesus.
- The church meets the needs of people.

- God wants people to gather to worship Him.
- The money people give at church is called tithes and offerings.
- The Lord's Supper is a special event at church. People can remember Jesus when they see the Lord's Supper being observed.
- Baptism shows that people have trusted in Jesus as Savior.

Bible-Learning Activities

God wants people to gather to worship Him.

Ask your young elementary student, "What does God want from us?" I (Ken) know that if I started my day asking the Lord that question, my day most likely would go much better. What does God want from us? God doesn't need anything from us; however, God does want a relationship with us. God loves us and delights in our worship of Him. God also is pleased when His people gather and worship Him together in unity. God created us to worship. Help your child learn this Bible verse that I memorized as a child: "I rejoiced with those who said to me, 'Let's go to the house of the LORD'" (Ps. 122:1).

The Lord's Supper is a special event at church. People can remember Jesus when they see the Lord's Supper being observed.

Work with your child to plan and prepare a simple family meal. As you are enjoying the meal, share with your child about Jesus and the special event called the Lord's Supper. Read Matthew 26:17–19, 26–30 together. Ask your elementary child the following questions: "Who were Jesus' friends at the special meal? Why was this meal special? What kind of food do you think Jesus and His friends ate?" Allow your child to also ask questions. Next, read 1 Corinthians 11:24–25 and explain that Jesus wants people at church to remember Him when they observe the Lord's Supper.

Teaching Middle Elementary Kids about the Church

What are your earliest memories of church? Did you start going to church as a child, teenager, adult? As parents, we want to instill in our kids a love for Jesus and His bride the church. The following statements and activities are designed to help you with that task.

Biblical Concept Statements

- A church is a group of Christians who meet together to worship and serve God.
- Churches set apart people to do certain tasks.
- God uses the church to meet the needs of people in the community and around the world.
- God wants people to gather to worship Him.
- In addition to money, offerings can include time, talents, and possessions.
- The Lord's Supper is a way to remind people about what Jesus did. Christians participate in the Lord's Supper.
- Baptism by immersion shows that people have trusted Jesus as Savior and Lord.

Bible-Learning Activities

In addition to money, offerings can include time, talents, and possessions.

Open your Bible and ask your child to read Malachi 3:10. Discuss the difference between a tithe and an offering. A *tithe* is 10 percent of our earnings, while an offering is anything more than that amount. Does your child receive an allowance or extra money for doing chores? If so, encourage him to give God a tithe of that allowance. In so doing, your elementary student will develop a life-long habit of giving. Offerings we give God are not always monetary. Help your child clean out his closet and clothes drawers. Go with your child to deliver out-grown clothes that are in good condition to a local charity or your church's clothes closet. Explain that your child's gift of clothes is an offering.

Baptism by immersion shows that people have trusted Jesus as Savior and Lord.

Read with your child the account of Jesus' baptism in Matthew 3:13–17. Talk about why Jesus was baptized by immersion. Define *immersion* in this context as Jesus' being lowered under the water's surface. Read Romans 6:4 and share that baptism by immersion is a picture of Jesus' burial and resurrection. Jesus chose to be baptized in this way to set an example for all Christians. Next, talk about the Ethiopian's baptism in Acts 8:26–39. Emphasize that baptism doesn't save us from sin, only Jesus saves.

Teaching Preteens about the Church

Regardless of how you may feel, you are still a strong influence in your preteen's life. The priority you place on regular, active church attendance and ministry positively influences the trajectory of your child's spiritual health.[1] Your almost-teenager is developing faith patterns while watching you—patterns that can influence their lives as the future parents of your grandchildren.

Biblical Concept Statements

- The church is a fellowship of baptized believers who meet together to worship and serve God. Churches today are part of the movement Jesus and His followers began.
- God calls church leaders to train believers to do God's work.
- God uses the church to meet people's needs as an expression of His love.
- Churches gather together to worship and respond to God.
- God wants people to be good stewards of their money, time, talents, and possessions.
- The Lord's Supper is an ordinance—a command Jesus gave to the church. The body and blood of Jesus are represented in the Lord's Supper. Christians participate in the Lord's Supper to remember Jesus' death.
- Baptism is an ordinance—a command Jesus gave to the church. Baptism by immersion is a symbol of Jesus' death, burial, and resurrection. Christians

are baptized to show they have trusted in Jesus as
Savior and Lord.

Bible Conversation Starters

*God uses the church to meet people's needs as an
expression of His love.*

Many churches wait until kids are teenagers before involving
them in Christian service. By that point, some kids have already
dropped out of church or are on the fringes of church attendance.
Schedule an appointment for you and your preteen to meet with a
church pastor or leader and talk about various local, state, national,
and global ministries your church supports. When your preteen
shows interest in a specific ministry opportunity, find ways your
almost-teenager can be involved in Christian service now.

*God wants people to be good stewards of their money,
time, talents, and possessions.*

Fold a sheet of paper twice to make a two-by-two grid. Next,
instruct your preteen to label each quadrant with one of these
words: *money, time, talents, possessions.* Lead your child to make a
list of what she possesses in each of the four squares. For example,
your almost-teen may list something like this in each quadrant:
$15.00, 12 hours, storyteller, game console. Guide your preteen
to read the story of famine relief in Acts 11:27–30. Discuss with
your student needs she can help meet with the items she listed on
her paper.

Teaching Middle Schoolers about the Church

There is so much for your middle schooler to learn about church. There is even more to learn about the local church in your community. However, the suggestions below will focus on the church described in the Bible.

Biblical Concept Statements

- The church is a fellowship of believers, and we are called to meet together regularly.
- The church is not a place or a building but consists of the people who belong to the family of God.
- The church is responsible for training and equipping its members for works of ministry, and church members are called to give of their time, resources, and talents.
- The ordinances of the church are the Lord's Supper and baptism, which are earthly symbols of eternal realities.

Bible Conversation Starters

The church is a fellowship of believers, and we are called to meet together regularly.

I encourage you to make sure your middle schooler has a good understanding that the church is not about a building. The church is about followers of Jesus. In fact, the church belongs to Jesus as His bride. The church building will one day cease to exist, but the church itself is eternal. Read the entire 12th chapter of Romans with your teenager. Discuss the similarities and differences of your church and the New Testament church as described in the verses you just read. Pray, asking God to use your family to help your church be what God desires it to be.

The church is responsible for training and equipping its members for works of ministry, and church members are called to give of their time, resources, and talents.

Guide your middle schooler to read Exodus 25:1–9; 35:4–9, 20–35; and 36:1–7. Make a list of some of the items people gave as offerings for the building of the tabernacle. Lead your young teen to discover this pattern of giving: 1) God through Moses requested an offering for a specific purpose; 2) people donated their possessions, time, and skills; and 3) people kept giving until Moses told them to stop. Discuss with your student how that giving pattern is applicable to her and to your church.

Teaching High Schoolers about the Church

I really get excited when we turn the page to our high schoolers. I get excited when I see God's hand at work in their young lives. Such potential. As your high schooler moves closer to young adulthood, please make sure he or she has a good understanding of the following principles related to what the Bible says about the church.

Biblical Concept Statements

- The church is a community of believers who are called to meet together regularly to study Scripture, pray, worship, serve and encourage one another, and proclaim the gospel to the world.

- The church is not a place or a building but is made up of the people who belong to the family of God, and whereas under the Old Covenant, God dwelled in the temple or the tabernacle, today God dwells in His people and works through them to advance His kingdom.
- The church is called to train and equip its members for works of ministry, including giving their time, resources, and talents to serve those within the church and reach those outside the church.
- The ordinances of the church are the Lord's Supper, which represents the body and blood of Jesus as the payment of our sin, and baptism, which represents our sharing in Jesus' burial and resurrection.

Bible Conversation Starters

The church is a community of believers who are called to meet together regularly to study Scripture, pray, worship, serve and encourage one another, and proclaim the gospel to the world.

As an older teen, your child's view of the local church is probably not as idealized as it once was. Unfortunately, many teens have become disillusioned with church after observing unchristian behavior in a heated church business meeting, or after experiencing the termination of a beloved student minister. Help your student navigate those difficult times by reminding him that regardless of how others act, the church is still the bride of Christ. And, as Christ followers we are to serve Jesus through the church.

The church is called to train and equip its members for works of ministry, including giving their time, resources, and talents to serve those within the church and reach those outside the church.

The Bible teaches that the church is to train and "equip the saints for the work of ministry" (Eph. 4:12). For greater context, read through Ephesians 4:1–16 with your high schooler. Engage in an honest discussion about how your church follows or doesn't follow the model prescribed in these verses. Talk about ways your family can "walk worthy of the calling you have received" (Eph. 4:1) and contribute to unity in your church through ministry opportunities in both your church and community.

Digging Deeper in Biblical Truth

Use the statements below to help your high schooler think deeply about the Church and to be prepared to defend his beliefs.

Being: When we are brought into God's family by faith, we become part of a family who is connected for the sake of loving, supporting, correcting, and encouraging one another.

Doing: Because we are part of a family, God's church, we should prioritize spending time together, and we should sacrificially serve one another.

Apologetic: Many today believe we can have a relationship with God without belonging to a church. Whereas going to church is not what saves us, we belong to a church not only to worship corporately and to be fed but also to serve the needs of others. When we fail to engage with our church family, we are not following Christ in serving sacrificially.

13

Teaching My Family God's Plan of Salvation

When I (Ken) was eight years old, I had a transformational experience. I prayed, placing my trust in Jesus and confessing Him as my Savior and Lord. I remember that day just like it was yesterday. It was an experience that changed my life forever.

Read the Bible

Read Ephesians 2:1–10 and observe the beautiful picture of salvation Paul describes. Look again at verse 8: "For you are saved by grace through faith, and this is not from yourselves; it is God's gift" (Eph. 2:8). Did you catch that? Salvation is a *gift*. We can't earn it. According to Romans 6:23, the only thing we can earn is death and eternal separation from God the Father.

Think about the Bible

Salvation is a process that God initiates through conviction of sin by the Holy Spirit. Salvation is the ultimate reason why we teach biblical truth to our kids. The goal of every biblical concept statement we've looked at so far is to point our children to Jesus and His saving power. Are you prepared to share the message of salvation with your child? If not, relax, take a deep breath and continue reading. I am here to help. In the coming pages I will offer you several suggestions, a few Bible verses, and some ideas on how to teach your preschooler, elementary child, preteen, middle schooler, and high school student about salvation and the transformation that it brings.

Teaching Younger Preschoolers about Salvation

What should be our approach when teaching younger preschoolers about salvation? My advice is to plan for the result and teach foundational biblical truth. Your child will not always be this age, preschoolers grow so fast! Your young child will reach a point in her spiritual maturity where she can place her faith in Jesus as her Savior and Lord. Everything you teach is pointing your child toward that beginning point of her discipleship journey.

Biblical Concept Statements

- God loves us.
- God cares about us.

Bible-Learning Activities

God loves us.

As you cuddle, diaper, or bathe your infant or toddler, say, "God loves us, and God loves _____ [insert your child's name]." Repeat a few times, inserting the names of family members and friends in the blank. This places the familiar sound of your voice into the mind of your child while teaching the biblical truth that God loves each one of us.

God cares about us.

Explain to your preschooler that God cares about every part of you. God cares about your toes and your feet. God cares about your legs and knees. God cares about your tummy. God cares about your head, lips, and nose. Touch each part of the body as you refer to it. Your younger preschooler will be learning that God cares about them from the top of their head to the bottom of their feet!

Teaching Middle Preschoolers about Salvation

Continue building foundations for salvation in your preschooler's life by teaching your child fundamental biblical truth about God and Jesus.

Biblical Concept Statements
- God sent Jesus because He loves us.
- God sent Jesus because He cares about us.
- People make wrong choices.

Bible-Learning Activities

God sent Jesus because He loves us and cares about us.

Explain to your preschooler that God loves them. Tell them God loves them so much, He sent Jesus. Open your Bible and read John 3:16 with your preschooler. Explain that God must love us a lot, if He loved us enough to send His son.

People make wrong choices.

Parents often unintentionally offer their preschoolers impractical choices. Make sure you ask your two- or three-year-old to choose between choices you are willing to honor. For example, instead of asking, "Do you want to stay here by yourself?" ask, "Do you want Granddaddy or Grams to take you to the car?" Even children not talking yet can indicate their response to some choices. Point out that God created your child to make choices.

Teaching Older Preschoolers about Salvation

Most older preschoolers are still in the foundation-building state of salvation and are not yet ready to receive God's gift of eternal life. That's okay. Keep teaching your preschooler biblical concepts and praying that when the Holy Spirit convicts your child of sin, he or she will respond favorably.

Biblical Concept Statements

- God sent Jesus to help people because He loves them.
- God sent His only Son, Jesus, because He cares about us.
- People choose to disobey God.

Bible-Learning Activities

God sent Jesus to help people because He loves them.

Ask: "Who is God? Who is Jesus? Where do God and Jesus live? Did you know that God sent Jesus to the earth because He loves us?" Read John 3:16. Feel free to paraphrase the verse: "God so loved the world that He gave His Son." Highlight the verse in your child's Bible with a yellow crayon, and guide your preschooler to remember the words of the verse and what they mean.

God sent His only Son, Jesus, because He cares about us.

Ask: "How do we know that God cares for us?" Prompt your preschooler with ideas such as, "God gives us good food to eat. God gives us a place to live. God gives us clothes to wear. God gives us a mommy and/or a daddy to help us." Point out that the best way we know God loves is the fact that God sent His only Son to the earth. Say, "The prophet Isaiah wrote in the Bible, 'God will send a child to be born' (Isa. 7:14). Isaiah was talking about Jesus!"

Teaching Younger Elementary Kids about Salvation

The Holy Spirit may begin prompting your six- or seven-year-old and convicting her of sin. Remember, though, that God saves individuals at various ages and stages of development. Try not to be stressed if your child shows no interest in trusting Jesus as her Savior and Lord. Just keep teaching foundational truth and praying for your child.

Biblical Concept Statements

- God provided a way for people to become Christians because He loves them.
- God sent His only Son, Jesus, to be the only Savior of the world.
- Sin is choosing my way and disobeying God.
- Jesus took the punishment for people's sins.

- People who trust Jesus as their Savior and Lord are Christians.
- God will forgive people when they ask Him.

Bible-Learning Activities

Sin is choosing my way and disobeying God.

Ask: "What does it mean to disobey? What happens when you disobey? Who gets hurt when you disobey? Have you ever chosen to disobey God? Do you know what disobeying God is called?" Define *sin* as, "actions, attitudes, words, or thoughts that do not please God."[1] Ask your child if she has sinned, and if so, ask her what "sins" she can identify. If your young elementary child doesn't understand what sin is nor recognize it in her own life, she may not be ready to become a Christian since repenting of sin is part of the salvation process.

People who trust Jesus as their Savior and Lord are Christians.

Children this age who have grown up going to church often say, "I want to be baptized." However, your child may just want to go swimming in the baptistry. Ask probing questions and be ready to define terms, such as *savior, Christian,* and *baptize.* State, "A *savior* is someone who saves others from something. God sent Jesus to save us from our sin and eternity in hell. Jesus is the only Person who can save us." Mention that a *Christian* is someone who confesses Jesus as his Savior and Lord. Explain that *baptize* means, "to lower someone in the water and bring him back up. The person who is baptized is following Jesus' example by showing others that he has confessed Jesus as Savior and Lord."[2] If your child is not ready to become a Christian, that's okay. Keep the conversation open and be ready to answer your elementary student's questions.

Teaching Middle Elementary Kids about Salvation

Eight- and nine-year-olds are curious and ask a lot of questions. Be prepared to use the following biblical concept statements for the critical questions they may ask about salvation. Also, be ready to talk through "Appendix A: The Gospel, God's Plan for Me."

Biblical Concept Statements

- God provided a plan for salvation because He loves me.
- Salvation is the beginning of a growing relationship with Jesus that lasts forever. Through salvation, my sin is forgiven and the gift of eternal life with God begins.
- The punishment for sin is separation from God.
- Jesus died to pay the penalty for all my sins—past, present, and future.
- God's salvation is a gift that every person needs and can receive.
- When the Holy Spirit convicts me of my sin, I can turn away from my sin (repent) and trust Jesus as my personal Savior.

Bible-Learning Activities

God provided a plan for salvation because He loves me.

Share that God provided a way for people to become Christians through the life, death, burial, and resurrection of His Son, Jesus. Ask: "Why do you think God did that for you?" Help your child discover the answer by reading John 3:16 and Romans 5:8 in her Bible. Say, "God sent Jesus to save us because God loves us and has a plan for us." Encourage your elementary student to mark those two verses in her Bible and memorize them.

Jesus died to pay the penalty for all my sins—past, present, and future.

Helping your child understand why Jesus had to die is critical to the process of their spiritual maturation. Read with your elementary student Hebrews 9:22 and Romans 6:23. Talk about the price for sin, including the pouring out of Jesus' blood when He died on the cross. Explain that Jesus died to pay the penalty for all our sins. He died to pay the price for the sins we committed in the past. He died to pay the price for the sins we are committing now. And He died to pay the price for the sins we will commit in the future.

Teaching Preteens about Salvation

Whether or not your preteen has already received God's gift of salvation through Jesus Christ, the following discipleship statements will be helpful as you navigate the topic of salvation.

Biblical Concept Statements

- God had a plan for salvation before the beginning of time.
- Jesus willingly died to provide salvation. Jesus' death and resurrection make salvation possible.
- The punishment for sin is eternal death and hell.
- People cannot save themselves. Jesus died to pay the penalty for our sins, redeeming and rescuing us from sin and death.
- God's salvation is eternal. Nothing can separate Christians from God's love.
- A growing relationship with Jesus is important and necessary. A Christian experiences joy when he recognizes God is working in his life and in the lives of others

Bible Conversation Starters

Jesus willingly died to provide salvation. Jesus' death and resurrection make salvation possible.

Ask: "Why did Jesus have to die? Whose fault is it that Jesus died? Why didn't Jesus tell the angels to rescue Him?" For answers to these and other questions your preteen may have, spend some time with your almost-teenager reading and discussing Isaiah 53. Point out that this passage is talking about the suffering servant and is viewed as a prophecy of Jesus' suffering. Next, read Matthew 26:36–56. Explain that Jesus chose to die for us because that was the only way we could be reconciled to our Holy God. Celebrate with your child that Jesus rose from the dead and that Christians will live with Him forever.

A growing relationship with Jesus is important and necessary. A Christian experiences joy when he recognizes God is working in his life and in the lives of others.

Just as your preteen is experiencing a major growth spurt physically, your student may also experience a growth spurt spiritually. Ask your preteen the best way to get to know a new friend, and your child will tell you the answer is to spend time with that individual. (Of course, your kid may equate texting and communicating via social media as "spending time" with someone.) Mention that if your preteen wants to have a closer relationship with Jesus, he needs to spend time reading the Bible and praying. (Obviously, Jesus doesn't text or send messages on social media.) A crucial component to your almost-teenager's development as a Christ follower is reading the Bible. Your preteen will be excited when he experiences the Word of the Lord at work in his life.

Teaching Middle Schoolers about Salvation

By this age, I (Ken) pray your middle schooler has a good understanding of the overall concept of salvation. That understanding comes from a personal relationship with Jesus Christ that is grounded in biblical truth. Remember, learning is a process for all teenagers. The following suggestions may offer help as you answer your middle schooler's questions.

Biblical Concept Statements

- Before the beginning of time, God's plan for salvation centered on Jesus' death and resurrection.

- People cannot save themselves, and Jesus is the only way to be reconciled to God.
- Because of our rebellion against God, we deserve eternal punishment.
- God's salvation is eternal, and nothing can separate us from Him.
- We can be confident in our salvation when we live in obedience to God and in ways that reflect Jesus.

Bible Conversation Starters

People cannot save themselves, and Jesus is the only way to be reconciled to God.

Help your middle schooler understand that no matter what your student does or doesn't do, your child cannot save himself from the penalty of sin. Only God, through the blood of Jesus, can save your young teenager from the penalty of sin. Read Romans 5:6–11. Make sure your middle schooler understands that Jesus died to pay the price for his sin. Jesus died to rescue your student from sin and eternal death, and to restore your young teenager's relationship with God the Father. Engage your middle schooler in a deeper conversation by asking, "Why do you need to be saved from sin and death? Why is Jesus the only Person who could pay the price for your sin? Why should a person want to spend eternity with God and Jesus?" These and other *why* questions will help your middle schooler mature spiritually and will prepare him to defend his faith.

God's salvation is eternal, and nothing can separate us from Him.

Stop. Read that statement again. Those eleven words may be some of the most important words your middle schooler needs to hear. Why? Kids who become Christians as seven-, eight-, and nine-year-olds often doubt their salvation during the teen years. Help your student understand that nothing he does can erase his salvation experience. Encourage your young teenager to underline or highlight these verses in his Bible: "My sheep hear my voice, I know them, and they follow me. I give them eternal life, and they will never perish. No one will snatch them out of my hand. My Father, who has given them to me, is greater than all. No one is able to snatch them out of the Father's hand" (John 10:27–29). Continue the conversation as long and as often as necessary.

Teaching High Schoolers about Salvation

I pray your high school student is living a transformed life made possible by the saving blood of Jesus Christ. Growing in his or her faith and sharing the good news of Jesus with others is critical. Provide encouragement and a listening ear as your teenager continues to experience the blessing of salvation.

Biblical Concept Statements

- Before the beginning of time, God's plan for salvation centered on Jesus' death and resurrection, which make salvation possible.

- No amount of good works can save a person, and Jesus' paying the penalty for our sin is the only way to be reconciled to God.
- Because of rebellion against God, all people are cut off from a relationship with Him and deserve eternal death and hell, which is the punishment for sin.
- God's salvation is eternal, and once we are adopted into God's family, nothing can separate us from Him.
- We can be confident in our salvation when we, as a matter of desire, live in obedience to God and in ways that reflect Jesus.

Bible Conversation Starters

No amount of good works can save a person, and Jesus' paying the penalty for our sin is the only way to be reconciled to God.

The idea that we can earn our way into heaven by doing good things has been popularized by music, books, and movies. The antithesis to this thinking is the widely held false belief that if we do too many bad things, we're destined for hell. Neither is biblical. Read Romans 8:1–11 with your high schooler. Talk about how only God through the blood of Jesus can save us from the penalty of sin. On the other hand, a blatant rejection of Jesus will result in spending an eternity in hell. The pressure is off. Good works don't save us, and wrong choices don't prevent us from receiving God's gift of forgiveness and eternal life. However, that doesn't mean we can do whatever we want to do. People who trust in Jesus have a desire to follow Him and live according to God's Word.

God's salvation is eternal, and once we are adopted into God's family, nothing can separate us from Him.

If your child became a Christian in elementary school, the probability of her doubting her salvation as a teenager is high. This is normal. Walk through her salvation experience with her, asking questions and helping your teenager recall the circumstances that led to her trusting in Jesus. Next, spend time together reading the following Scripture passages: Romans 10:13; 1 John 1:8–9; 2:3–6; 3:14; 4:13; and 5:13. Assure your teen that if she truly received God's gift of eternal life, then her salvation is secure. However, only your high schooler can know for sure if she is a Christian. Read Romans 8:38–39 together and pray that God will either convict your high schooler of her need for salvation or give her assurance that she is a Christian. If your student continues to struggle, encourage, listen to, and pray for her.

Digging Deeper in Biblical Truth

Use the statements below to help your high schooler think deeply about salvation and to be prepared to defend his beliefs.

Being: Because salvation is a gift from God and has been secured by the sacrifice of Christ, we become children of God forever when we surrender to Him in faith and turn away from sin.

Doing: Though we cannot work to earn salvation, true faith is evidenced in how we live. Therefore, we should seek to know and do all that God commands.

Apologetic: Many people believe we will go to heaven as a matter of works—because they try to be good people, because they pray, or because they simply believe God exists. However, true salvation cannot be earned and comes only by faith in Jesus.

Part 3

HOW CAN MY CHURCH PARTNER WITH ME?

14

Partnering with the Church

In my (Ken's) youngest, most formative years, I attended Fayette First Baptist Church in Fayette, Alabama. Mrs. Lowery, a faithful children's ministry volunteer, rocked me and shared with me the foundational truths of Scripture, namely that God loves me. She didn't worry that I was too young to understand. She didn't give up because it seemed I wasn't completely understanding God's truth. Instead, Mrs. Lowery *taught* me. She sang songs, embedding biblical knowledge in my brain. She continually reminded me that God loves me, God made me, and God has a purpose for me. Mrs. Lowery understood what the writer of Hebrews meant when he said, "You need someone to teach you the basic principles of God's revelation again. You need milk, not solid food" (Heb. 5:12).

Because of people like Mrs. Lowery who discipled me, I have graduated to solid spiritual food. But that would not be the case if first I hadn't been fed the milk of foundational Bible truth. We all build knowledge upon prior learning. We learn to recognize numbers before we add them together. We discover words before we string them together in a sentence. The same is true with learning the Bible. We learn about Who God is before we begin to understand His creative work and His plan to rescue us from sin through His Son Jesus.

By now you realize that the Levels of Biblical Learning are a picture of how biblical truths build from very simple concepts to more complex realities. Therefore, I cannot overemphasize the importance of teaching God's Word to infants and toddlers both at home and at church. When a teacher rocks an infant at church and tells her God loves her, that adult is partnering with parents to teach biblical truth found in Bible verses such as these:

> But you, Lord, are a compassionate and gracious God, slow to anger and abounding in faithful love and truth. (Ps. 86:15)

> Give thanks to the God of heaven! His faithful love endures forever. (Ps. 136:26)

> The LORD appeared to him from far away. I have loved you with an everlasting love; therefore, I have continued to extend faithful love to you. (Jer. 31:3)

> "For God loved the world in this way: He gave his one and only Son, so that everyone who believes in him will not perish but have eternal life." (John 3:16)

> "No one has greater love than this: to lay down his life for his friends." (John 15:13)

> I have been crucified with Christ, and I no longer live, but Christ lives in me. The life I now live in

the body, I live by faith in the Son of God, who
loved me and gave himself for me. (Gal. 2:20)

But, how can kids master complex truths of Scripture if they
don't learn simple concepts as preschoolers? While knowledge does
build on prior learning, elementary kids and teenagers typically
approach biblical learning with an age-appropriate vocabulary
and a limited ability to start thinking abstractly. So, while youth
teachers may tell a thirteen-year-old that God loves him, they
don't necessarily teach an entire lesson with that as their primary
objective. Instead, they build on how God designed that young
teenager to learn. Doing so allows adults to move teens quickly to
the fuller truth that God loves all people, regardless of ethnicity
or status, and proved His love by sending Jesus to bear the penalty
for their sin on the cross.

Through God the Father's love, God the Son's sacrifice, and
God the Holy Spirit's guidance, parents and teachers at church
can be part of discipling babies, preschoolers, elementary students,
preteens, and teenagers. Furthermore, the discipleship process can
start at any age. Knowing this, what does a discipleship partnership between the church and home look like? Let's try to answer
that question by asking and answering three additional questions.

First, what is the discipleship plan for the church's preschool,
elementary, preteen, and student ministries? I'm not talking about
a well-articulated mission statement, while that can be important
for setting the overall ministry direction. Church leaders need to
be able to show parents a blueprint of spiritual progression that
church staff and teachers follow. That can be as simple as sharing
with parents the Levels of Biblical Learning in the form of this
book, a booklet, a poster, or a web page.

That's right. The Levels of Biblical Learning can serve as your church's discipleship plan. Bellevue Baptist Church in Cordova, Tennessee, where I (Ken) serve, received permission from Lifeway to publish a customized Levels of Biblical Learning booklet specifically designed for our church family. In this way, we have helped our leaders, teachers, and parents acquire a sense of ownership of the discipleship process.

Second, what is the strategy for implementing the discipleship plan for babies through eighteen-year-olds? For me (Landry) an indicator of a clearly defined discipleship strategy is the existence of an ongoing curriculum map for the primary Bible-teaching time (Sunday School, Life Groups, Children's Church, Kids' Service, Student Worship, etc.). Conversely, a haphazard approach to curriculum planning often points to the absence of a real plan to discipline kids and students.

One of the characteristics of a good Bible study plan, or scope and sequence, is that it covers at least one year of Bible content. Some curricula have two- or three-year plans, or even longer in some cases. Balance is another trait of a good scope and sequence. This type of Bible study plan includes all of the Bible's major teachings. Without such a plan, churches often default to a kids or student ministry leader's favorite Bible stories and passages. That approach is akin to eating only dessert for dinner every night, instead of eating a well-balanced diet of proteins, grains, and vegetables.

Nonetheless, a strong scope and sequence is useless without quality curriculum materials that:

- Are Bible-based, Jesus-centered, doctrinally depend-
able, theologically sound, teacher-empowering,
family-engaging, and age-appropriate.
- Grow with kids and students by considering the
uniqueness of particular age groups.
- Engage preschoolers, elementary kids, preteens,
and teenagers through carefully crafted learning
activities. In fact, many of the activity ideas in
Part 2 of this book can be used in church settings.
- Equip the next generation of disciple makers.

Of course, an ongoing Bible study plan and accompanying
curriculum are not the only evidence of a family discipleship strategy. Another indicator is Vacation Bible School (VBS). According
to Lifeway Research, 64 percent of churches that offer VBS use
it as a tool to disciple kids within the church.[1] This makes sense,
considering the amount of concentrated time preschoolers and kids
participate in VBS. Melita Thomas, a VBS ministry specialist,
states, "A traditional VBS involves three hours a day for five days
in a row. This is equivalent of seven months of 'church' for today's
typical church-going child! The opportunities for evangelism,
discipleship and relationship-building that can take place in one
week of VBS might take half a year for a Sunday School teacher."[2]

The third question also concerns strategy: Is there a uniform
implementation strategy for babies through eighteen-year-olds?
So many times, a church's family discipleship ministry strategy
is actually comprised of two or more strategies. For example, a
church may have different plans for preschoolers, kids, middle
schoolers, and high school students. If the kids and student

ministries coordinate their primary Bible study curriculum, then they most likely have some sort of unified discipleship strategy.

Another way that churches work across age-groups for the purpose of family discipleship is observed in how major transitions are handled. How do preschoolers transition to the elementary children's ministry area? How are preteens assimilated into middle school ministry? How are middle schoolers moved to the high school area of ministry? What happens to new high school graduates? These transitions take place more smoothly when the leaders of each age-group ministry have a uniform discipleship strategy and are intentional in helping kids, students, and parents make these life changes in the context of both their homes and their church.

Additional ways churches choose to implement their strategies for discipling preschoolers, elementary kids, preteens, and teenagers may include spiritual mile-marker celebrations, special events, camps, short-term discipleship groups, and home resources. Churches that have a strategic family discipleship plan and implement that plan uniformly across all age groups understand the necessity of partnering with families in the essential work of discipleship.

15

Partnering with the Home

The apostle Peter encouraged his readers to "grow in the grace and knowledge of our Lord and Savior Jesus Christ" (2 Pet. 3:18). Those same words apply to all of us who trust in Jesus, adults and kids alike. Ultimately, kids and student ministry leaders want to see people grow spiritually. They want to come alongside parents and encourage children and teens to grow in biblical knowledge, love, and, most importantly, in their relationship with Jesus.

Ideally, this partnership occurs both at church and at home. Like many churches, the church where I (Ken) minister has chosen to intentionally partner with parents in the task of discipling their newborns, preschoolers, elementary kids, middle schoolers, and high school students. We have developed a discipleship journey that equips parents to engage their children in biblical truth. That journey is called, "Fight for Your Family." What makes this plan unique is the use of the Levels of Biblical Learning as the framework. "Fight for the Family" is part of our church's overall strategy for family discipleship. I suggest you create your own discipleship journey experience for families to implement in their homes, using an approach similar to this five-step process.

Step One: Prepare. Work with your church's senior pastor and other key leaders to create a plan that works best for your church and community context. Consider your family ministry philosophy, vision, mission, values, and goals.[1] Creating consistency from children's ministry all the way up through adult ministry helps families disciple their kids. Start from the understanding that families have various needs due to the different ages of their kids and students. A home with preschoolers operates differently than a home with high schoolers. A family with three school-age children looks vastly different than a home with a preschooler, a second grader, and a middle schooler.

I once heard a story about a farmer who was talking with his pastor after the Sunday morning message. The wise, kind-hearted farmer commented he had learned a long time ago that when he wanted to feed the cows, he didn't need to give them all the hay in the barn at once. We don't need to give families all the hay in the barn at once. Using the Levels of Biblical Learning as a guide, parents can teach their children digestible bites of Bible truth. Kids and teens might need a small amount at a time. The Levels of Biblical Learning gives everyone a different starting place. Some kids may stay in that starting place longer than others. On the other hand, they may understand their age-group's assigned biblical concept and are ready to jump to the next level. What is important is that discipleship is happening in the home.

Step Two: Provide. You may want to give your families copies of this book and encourage parents to use Part 2 for their family devotion times. Realizing that families also need "on-the-go" resources, my (Ken's) church provided parents with age-specific "battle plans" in the form of printed or digital cards. We produced separate battle plans for each of the ten weeks. Want to make your own cards? Rather than start from scratch, consider using content from each chapter in Part 2. For example, for week one you could focus on Creation and organize the cards using the outline already provided in chapter 4:

- Introduction of the Biblical Concept Area
- Read the Bible
- Think about the Bible
- Teach the Bible

Summarize the first three sections using bullet points. In the "Teach the Bible" section, choose just one or two activities families can do together. All the content should fit on the front and back of a five- by seven-inch card, or on just one side of a letter-size sheet of paper. And, there should be plenty of white space. Too many words may intimidate and discourage families. You will want to create one card for each age-group. Within each age-group, create ten cards, one for each of the ten concept areas.[2]

Step 3: Promote. Create a name for your church's discipleship journey experience. Begin promoting at least six weeks prior to the launch. Whatever mediums your local body of believers uses to get information out, use it! You may consider using print, public announcements, visuals, and giveaways. Make sure families receive the communication outside of the church walls via emails, texts, phone calls, and even postal mail. Then, make sure you are available to answer questions that arise.

Step 4: Party. Now let's get everyone excited about this new way to disciple kids and students! Consider rolling out the red carpet for a church-wide event where families are introduced to the Levels of Biblical Learning as the foundation of your church's family discipleship plan. Enlist the senior pastor or another prominent and respected church leader to encourage and challenge families. My (Ken's) church launched "Fight for Your Family" with a parent rally and then encouraged families to carve out one mealtime per week for ten weeks. During the meal, parents engage their children in Bible conversation. Each week for the ten weeks, families focus on one of the ten biblical concept areas of the Levels of Biblical Learning.

Step 5: Perpetuate. The discipleship journey we've been talking about is only part of a church's overarching family discipleship plan. We've all heard of churches with great family ministry ideas that started strong and fizzled out after a few weeks or months. A sustainable family discipleship ministry is more than a ten-week campaign. It's a week-in-week-out endeavor that requires hard work and mutual accountability on the part of churches and individual families. However, a plan that has behind it a solid strategy, practical tools, and senior leadership support can be successful and God-honoring.

Because the Levels of Biblical Learning is built on the idea that children are capable of growing in all of these areas as they develop, parents and churches can use this tool to track a child's growth from their earliest childhood years to their earliest adult years. Remember, though, that spiritual development is a daily process. There is no formula. It is not a checkbox system. We (Ken, Jana, and Landry) look forward to seeing what the Lord has in store for you, your family, and your church family in the days ahead.

Conclusion

R emember those kids in three different age groups from the Introduction? They are all now teenagers, still growing in their faith. Our (Jana's family) devotionals look a little different these days than they did even just a year ago. We've gone from using guided devotionals to straight up Scripture, studying books of the Bible in-depth.

We could not have done this without children's and youth ministries that value age-appropriate learning, encouraging us to partner with them at home. In our home, we still reference the Levels of Biblical Learning and are grateful that this tool now includes two new levels for student ministry.

As my teenagers continue to grow and eventually leave our nest, it will comfort me knowing that they have a firm foundation in the Lord. Our Heavenly Father has been so faithful in every age and every stage of our kids' childhood. They are still learning and still growing in their faith, and I have now moved on to the parenting books about raising teens!

More than anything, I continue to cherish all the stages of spiritual development that my children have gone through. I pray that the families introduced to the Levels of Biblical Learning will discover the true joy of introducing their little ones to Jesus, teaching foundational truth, and ultimately walking with their kids and teens in their faith journey.

APPENDIX

Appendix A

The Gospel, God's Plan for Me

The word *gospel* means "good news." It is the message about Christ, the kingdom of God, and salvation. Use the following guide to share the gospel with your kids and teens.

God rules. The Bible tells us God created everything, including you and me, and He is in charge of everything (Gen. 1:1; Rev. 4:11; Col. 1:16–17).

We sinned. Since the time of Adam and Eve, everyone has chosen to disobey God (Rom. 3:23). The Bible calls this sin. Because God is holy, God cannot be around sin. Sin separates us from God and deserves God's punishment of death (Rom. 6:23).

God provided. God sent His Son, Jesus, the perfect solution to our sin problem, to rescue us from the punishment we deserve. It's something we, as sinners, could never earn on our own. Jesus alone saves us (John 3:16; Eph. 2:8–9).

Jesus gives. Jesus lived a perfect life, died on the cross for our sins, and rose again. Because Jesus gave up His life for us, we can be welcomed into God's family for eternity. This is the best gift ever! (Rom. 5:8; 2 Cor. 5:21; 1 Pet. 3:18).

We respond. We can respond to Jesus. The ABCs of Becoming a Christian is a simple tool that helps us remember how to respond when prompted by the Holy Spirit to receive the gift Jesus offers.

Admit to God that you are a sinner. The first people God created chose to sin and disobey God. Ever since then, all people have chosen to sin and disobey (Rom. 3:23). Tell God you messed up and you are sorry for doing your own thing, and turning away from Him through your thoughts, words, and actions. Repent, turning away from your sin (Acts 3:19; 1 John 1:9). Repenting doesn't just mean turning from doing bad things to doing good things; it means turning from sin and even from your own good works, and turning to Jesus, trusting only in Him to save you.

Believe that Jesus is God's Son and receive God's gift of forgiveness from sin. You must believe that only Jesus can save you, and you cannot save yourself from your sin problem—not even by praying to God, going to church, or reading your Bible. Your faith or your trust is only in Jesus and what He did for you through His life, death, and resurrection (Acts 4:12; 16:31; John 14:1, 6; Eph. 2:8–9).

Confess your faith in Jesus Christ as Savior and Lord. Tell God and tell others what you believe. If Jesus is your Savior, you are trusting only in Him to save you. Jesus is also Lord, which means He is in charge. You can start following Him and doing what He says in the Bible. You are born again into a new life and look forward to being with God forever (Rom. 10:9–10, 13).

If you sense that your child is under conviction from the Holy Spirit and is ready to respond to the good news that is the gospel, spend some time talking, listening, and praying with your child. If you sense that your child is not ready to pray and respond in faith and repentance, continue to prayerfully teach your child about Jesus, using the Levels of Bible Learning and suggestions in this book.

Appendix B

Foundational Bible Stories by Concept Area

To specify a Bible story as *foundational* is in many ways a subjective exercise. After all, every story in the Bible is important and is included in the canon of Scripture for a reason. Nonetheless, for our purposes, the term *foundational Bible story* refers to a story that is central to the spiritual growth of your children. However, our list is certainly not exhaustive.

We have attempted to organize the following 90 stories by biblical concept area. Needless to say, some of these stories could fall under more than one concept, thereby making the categorization of stories subjective as well. And, some of these stories may be easier for preteens and teenagers to understand than for preschoolers and elementary kids.

CREATION

God Created the World
Genesis 1:1–2:3

Adam and Eve's Sin
Genesis 2:15; 3

Cain and Abel
Genesis 4:1–16

Noah and the Ark
Genesis 6:5–9:17

BIBLE

The Ten Commandments
Exodus 19:3–6; 20:1–17

Josiah and the Lost Scroll
2 Kings 22

Ezra Read the Law
Nehemiah 8:1–12; Ezra 7:6–10

Jeremiah Wrote God's Words
Jeremiah 36:1–4, 22–24, 27–28, 32

Jesus Read the Bible Scroll
Luke 4:16–28

Timothy Learned about God
1 Timothy 1

GOD

The Sacrifice of Isaac
Genesis 22:1–18

The Israelites Crossed the Red Sea
Exodus 14

Joshua and Caleb Obeyed God
Numbers 13–14

Joshua and Jericho
Joshua 6:1–21

God Chose Gideon
Judges 6:12–16; 7:1–8, 15–22

Samson
Judges 13–16

David and Goliath
1 Samuel 17:12–49

David Anointed King
2 Samuel 5

God Cared for Elijah
1 Kings 17:7–16

God Helped Elijah
1 Kings 18:2, 18–39

God Protected Elijah
1 Kings 19

Jesus Told the Parable of the Lost Son
Luke 15:11–32

JESUS

Prophets Told about Jesus
Isaiah 7:14; 9:6; Micah 5:2

Angels Visited Mary and Joseph
Matthew 1:18–25; Luke 1:26–38

Jesus Was Born
Luke 2:1–20

Simeon and Anna
Luke 2:25–38

Wise Men Worshiped Jesus
Matthew 2:1–12

Jesus Went to the Temple
Luke 2:41–50

John the Baptist
Matthew 3:1–12

Jesus Was Baptized
Matthew 3:13–17

Jesus Was Tempted
Matthew 4:1–11

Jesus Chose Twelve Helpers (Disciples)
Matthew 4:18–22; 10:2–4

Jesus Taught about Prayer
Matthew 6:5–15

Jesus Calmed the Storm
Matthew 8:23–27

Peter Walked on Water
Matthew 14:22–33

The Triumphal Entry
Matthew 21:1–11

The Last Supper
Matthew 26:17–30

Jesus Visited Mary and Martha
Luke 10:38–42

Jesus Healed Ten Lepers
Luke 17:11–19

Jesus and the Woman at the Well
John 4:1–26

Jesus Fed the 5,000
John 6:1–15

Jesus Healed a Blind Man
John 9:1–11, 35–39

Jesus Washed the Disciples' Feet
John 13:1–17

HOLY SPIRIT

The Ascension
Acts 1:1–11

The Holy Spirit Empowered Witnesses
Romans 8:14–16

The Fruit of the Spirit
Galatians 5:22–23

PEOPLE

Isaac Was Kind
Genesis 26:12–33

David and Jonathan
1 Samuel 18:1–5; 19:1–7; 20:1–42

Samuel's Birth and Calling
1 Samuel 1:20–28; 3

Elisha and the Widow
2 Kings 4:1–7

A Couple Helped Elisha
2 Kings 4:8–17

Esther
Esther 2–5

Daniel Obeyed God
Daniel 1:1–20

Daniel and the Lion's Den
Daniel 6

Jonah
Jonah 1–3

The Good Samaritan
Luke 10:25–37

FAMILY

Abram and Lot
Genesis 12:1–9; 13

Esau and Jacob
Genesis 27–28; 32:1–32; 33:1–4

Joseph and His Family
Genesis 37:1–36; 39:1–6; 41:1–45

Joseph Forgave His Brothers
Genesis 45:1–15; 50:15–21

Baby Moses
Exodus 2:1–10

Ruth's Family
Ruth 1–4

Hannah Prayed
1 Samuel 1:1–18

COMMUNITY AND WORLD

The Four Friends Brought a Man to Jesus
Mark 2:1–12

Paul, the Missionary
Acts 9:1–20; 13

Peter and Cornelius
Acts 10:9–43

Barnabas and Paul
Acts 13:13–52

Paul and Barnabas Disagreed
Acts 15:36–41

Lydia Learned about Jesus
Acts 16:11–15

Paul and Silas in Prison
Acts 16:16–34

Paul Taught in Athens
Acts 17:16–34

Priscilla and Aquila
Acts 18

Paul Taught in Rome
Acts 28

CHURCH

The Tabernacle
Exodus 35:1, 4–20; 36:1–38

Solomon and the Temple
1 Kings 8:1–61

Work Begins on the Temple
Ezra 3

A Woman Gave Her Money
Luke 21:1–4

The Church Began
Acts 2:1–40; Romans 8:14–16

The Church Grew
Acts 2:41–47

The Church Chose Leaders
Acts 6:1–7

Stephen Preached
Acts 6:8–15

Peter's Rescue
Acts 12:1–17

The Church in Corinth
1 Corinthians 1; 3; 4; 12

SALVATION

The Rich Young Ruler
Matthew 19:16–29

Jesus Prayed in the Garden
Matthew 26:36–46

Crucifixion and Resurrection
Matthew 27:27–61; 28:1–8

Zacchaeus Met Jesus
Luke 19:1–10

Thomas Believed
John 20:24–29

Breakfast with Jesus
John 21:1–13

Philip and the Ethiopian
Acts 8:26–31, 34–35, 38–39

Saul's Conversion
Acts 9:1–20

Appendix C

Supporting Bible Verses and Passages

One of the ways parents and teachers can help their pre-schoolers, elementary kids, preteens, and teenagers learn Bible truths is by teaching them the meanings of the following Bible verses and passages, and perhaps memorizing some of them as well.

CREATION

- ❑ Genesis 1:1–2
- ❑ Genesis 1:26
- ❑ Genesis 2:2
- ❑ Genesis 2:7
- ❑ Genesis 2:9
- ❑ Genesis 2:15
- ❑ Genesis 9:3
- ❑ Hebrews 11:3

BIBLE

- ❑ Isaiah 40:8
- ❑ John 20:31
- ❑ John 21:24

☐ Romans 1:1–4
☐ 2 Timothy 3:16–17
☐ 2 Peter 1:20–21

GOD

☐ Deuteronomy 6:4–5
☐ 1 Samuel 2:2
☐ Psalm 6:9
☐ Psalm 18:3
☐ Psalm 44:21
☐ Psalm 62:11
☐ Psalm 90:2
☐ Psalm 139:7–8
☐ Psalm 139:14
☐ Isaiah 12:5
☐ Isaiah 40:28
☐ Isaiah 61:8
☐ Matthew 3:16–17
☐ Matthew 5:48
☐ John 3:16
☐ Romans 1:25
☐ Romans 5:8
☐ Romans 8:28
☐ 1 Corinthians 10:31
☐ 2 Corinthians 1:20
☐ Philippians 1:11
☐ Philippians 4:19
☐ 1 Timothy 1:17
☐ 1 Peter 1:16
☐ 1 John 1:9

❏ 1 John 3:20
❏ 1 John 4:9
❏ 1 John 4:16

JESUS

❏ Genesis 3:15
❏ Isaiah 7:14
❏ Isaiah 9:6
❏ Isaiah 53:5
❏ Matthew 1:18–25
❏ Matthew 4:1–11
❏ Matthew 13:55
❏ Matthew 14:14
❏ Matthew 26:26–30
❏ Matthew 26:39
❏ Luke 2:46
❏ Luke 2:51–52
❏ Luke 23:34
❏ John 1:1, 14
❏ John 3:16
❏ John 4:25–26
❏ John 5:19
❏ John 8:58
❏ John 10:30
❏ John 11:25
❏ John 11:40–44
❏ John 14:6
❏ John 14:12
❏ John 14:15
❏ Acts 1:11

❑ Romans 5:8
❑ Romans 6:4
❑ Romans 8:34
❑ 1 Corinthians 15:20
❑ 2 Corinthians 5:17
❑ 2 Corinthians 5:21
❑ Colossians 1:16
❑ Hebrews 2:10–13
❑ Hebrews 4:15
❑ 1 John 4:14
❑ Revelation 1:18

HOLY SPIRIT

❑ Ezekiel 36:26–27
❑ John 14:16, 26
❑ John 15:26
❑ John 16:7–8
❑ John 16:12–13
❑ Acts 1:8
❑ Romans 8:2–6
❑ Romans 8:26
❑ 1 Corinthians 3:16
❑ 1 Peter 1:2
❑ 2 Peter 1:21

PEOPLE

❑ Genesis 1:27
❑ Deuteronomy 30:19
❑ Joshua 1:8
❑ 2 Chronicles 7:14

❑ Psalm 139:13–16
❑ Proverbs 1:7
❑ Proverbs 3:5–6
❑ Isaiah 41:10
❑ Jeremiah 1:5
❑ Jeremiah 29:11
❑ Matthew 6:14–15
❑ Mark 12:30
❑ John 14:15
❑ Acts 3:19
❑ Romans 12:6–8
❑ Romans 15:13
❑ 1 Corinthians 6:19–20
❑ 1 Corinthians 10:13
❑ 1 Corinthians 10:31
❑ 1 Corinthians 11:1
❑ 1 Corinthians 12:4–5
❑ Ephesians 4:32
❑ Philippians 4:8
❑ Colossians 3:13
❑ James 1:2
❑ James 5:16
❑ 1 Peter 4:10–11
❑ 2 Peter 1:3
❑ 2 Peter 3:18
❑ 1 John 4:16

FAMILY

❑ Genesis 1:27–28
❑ Genesis 31:3

- ❏ Exodus 20:12
- ❏ Deuteronomy 6:4–9
- ❏ Psalm 103:13
- ❏ Psalm 127:3–5
- ❏ Proverbs 22:6
- ❏ Matthew 19:6
- ❏ Ephesians 4:32
- ❏ Ephesians 5:23–25
- ❏ Ephesians 6:1–4
- ❏ Colossians 3:16
- ❏ 1 Timothy 5:8
- ❏ Hebrews 13:4
- ❏ James 1:27
- ❏ 1 Peter 2:5

COMMUNITY AND WORLD

- ❏ Genesis 1:27
- ❏ Psalm 139:13–14
- ❏ Matthew 28:19–20
- ❏ John 3:16
- ❏ John 15:17
- ❏ Acts 1:8
- ❏ Romans 10:15
- ❏ Romans 13:10
- ❏ 2 Corinthians 5:17
- ❏ Galatians 3:28

CHURCH

- ❏ Nehemiah 10:38
- ❏ Matthew 18:20

❏ Matthew 26:26–28
❏ Matthew 28:19
❏ Acts 10:48
❏ Romans 6:4
❏ Romans 12:10
❏ 1 Corinthians 11:23–24
❏ 1 Corinthians 11:26
❏ Ephesians 5:19–21
❏ Colossians 3:16
❏ 1 Timothy 5:17
❏ 1 Peter 4:10
❏ 1 Peter 5:1

SALVATION

❏ John 3:16
❏ Romans 5:8
❏ Romans 6:23
❏ Romans 8:39
❏ Romans 10:9
❏ 2 Corinthians 5:21
❏ Ephesians 1:4
❏ 1 Peter 2:2
❏ 1 Peter 5:7
❏ 1 John 1:9
❏ 1 John 4:16

Appendix D

Age-group Characteristics

As you read the following characteristics, you'll want to keep two things in mind: 1) This list is not exhaustive; 2) These are general statements and not every child will exhibit all of these characteristics. The purpose of our including this list is to give parents and teachers an idea of how God has wired kids to learn Bible truth.

Younger preschoolers are:

- developing a sense of trust as needs are met consistently
- sensing attitudes and expression of love
- growing in trust of adults
- beginning to distinguish between acceptable and unacceptable behaviors
- beginning to recognize simple pictures of Jesus
- singing simple songs about God and Jesus
- saying thank You to God
- listening to Bible stories

Middle preschoolers are:

- identifying some Bible people and stories

- understanding that God, Jesus, and the church are special
- beginning to develop a conscience and are sensitive to feelings of shame and guilt
- retelling Bible stories
- recognizing that God and Jesus love people and help people in special ways
- expressing love for God and Jesus

Older preschoolers are:

- remembering Bible stories
- retelling Bible stories
- recognizing how God and Jesus love people
- seeing how God helps people in special ways
- using the Bible to ask questions about God
- making life application of Bible verses
- seeing Jesus as a friend and a helper
- starting to make conclusions about God

Younger kids are:

- seeing Jesus as a friend and helper
- enjoying learning from the Bible
- beginning to have a simple understanding of sin
- seeing consequences to sin
- beginning to have a simple understanding of the gospel
- knowing the right answers but may not understand application
- interested in finding out more about God and Jesus and His plan of salvation

- using the Bible to ask questions about God
- making life application of Bible verses
- starting to make conclusions about God

Middle kids are:

- asking serious questions about religion
- developing values
- learning about being truthful and honest
- having difficulty making decisions
- beginning to feel the need for a Savior
- growing conscious of themselves and of sin
- wanting to do things the right way
- thinking in terms of right and wrong more than good and evil

Preteens are:

- developing concepts of love and trust
- hearing their conscience
- developing a value system
- forming concepts of personal worth
- seeking spiritual answers
- making many choices but may not follow through on long-term commitments
- feeling deeply about their own experiences
- beginning to adopt a religious belief system of their own

Middle schoolers are:

- continuing to develop core beliefs and values during these years

- beginning to think critically about their worldview and the worldviews of others
- dealing with issues surrounding identity and self-image
- asking questions about God's will for their lives
- learning the social and cultural norms in relationships
- developing a strong ability to connect biblical truths to life situations
- being taught the importance of having boundaries in all spheres of life
- learning to consistently practice spiritual disciplines

High schoolers are:

- comfortable in articulating their beliefs and values to those around them
- conscientiously aware and socially active regarding the cultural issues surrounding them
- asking how their faith is consistent or contradictory with other beliefs
- continuing to develop ideas pertaining to personal identity and self-image
- learning to navigate social and cultural norms in relationships
- exercising more independence and looking forward to life after high school
- learning fiscal responsibility through work and stewardship
- capable of exercising more leadership responsibilities within the church

Acknowledgements

So many people have spoken into the development of the ideas within the pages of this book and the Levels of Biblical Learning framework. With the fear of potentially omitting names of groups and individuals without whom this book would not be possible, we (Ken, Landry, and Jana) will try to thank the people who we know have contributed to the family discipleship plan described in these pages.

First, we want to thank Dr. Louis Hanks and Dr. Thomas Sanders for vision casting and pioneering the work that became known as the Levels of Biblical Learning. We also are grateful to the leaders and team members we serve at Bellevue Baptist Church, Cordova, Tennessee, and at Lifeway Christian Resources, Nashville, Tennessee. We are especially appreciative of the support of Taylor Combs, Dr. Bill Craig, Donna Gaines, Dr. Steve Gaines, Dr. Eric Geiger, Michael Kelley, Dr. Ben Mandrell, Logan Pyron and the B&H Publishing Team, Lifeway Kids Team, and Lifeway Students Team.

We are thankful for the many academicians and church leaders who have contributed to, taught, and implemented the Levels of Biblical Learning, including Steven Ackley, Jonathan Brown, Dr. Javier Elizondo, Dr. Jonathan Geukgeuzian, Dr. Kevin Jones, Dr. Timothy Paul Jones, Dr. Karen Kennemur, Kathy Kim, Dr. Diane Lane, Becky Marshall, Dr. Shelly Melia, Diane

Mitchell, Tonya O'Guinn, Dr. Donna Peavey, Dr. Jeanne Peter, Bianca Robinson, Tracy Ross, Emily Smith, and Dr. Currie Tilley.

Through the years, additional voices have spoken into the framework discussed in this book, including these former and current Lifeway colleagues: John Paul Basham, Mary Ann Bradberry, Rachel Coe, Brian Dembowczyk, Ann Edwards, Bill Emeott, Lauren Groves, Jen Hall, James Hargrave, Shelly Harris, Andrew Hudson, Lisa Jennette, Jeff Land, Cheryl Lewis, Becky Loyd, David Nelms, Angel Luis Ortiz, Chuck Peters, Tim Pollard, Dr. Lynn Pryor, Jeffrey Reed, Tracey Rogers, Debbie Ruth, Stephanie Salvatore, Kayla Stevens, Bekah Stoneking, Klista Storts, Dr. William Summey Jr., Melita Thomas, Ben Trueblood, Rhonda VanCleave, Dr. Trevin Wax, Mary Wiley, Scott Wiley, Delanee Williams, and Jerry Wooley.

Finally, we want to thank posthumously our dear friends Judy Latham, Cindy Lumpkin, and Jerry Vogel for their family discipleship legacy.

Notes

Chapter 1: Discipleship and the Levels of Biblical Learning

1. Information about the Levels of Biblical Learning, along with additional Bible-learning activities and conversation starters are found at lifeway.com/lobl.

2. See "Appendix B: Foundational Bible Stories by Concept Area" for a list of suggested Bible stories that help kids learn specific biblical concepts.

Chapter 2: Nothing Less than the Bible

1. Jana Magruder, *Nothing Less* (Nashville: Lifeway Christian Resources, 2017).

2. Lifeway Research, "Parent Adventure Study," 2007–08.

3. Lifeway Research, "Nothing Less Study," 2016.

4. For a list of suggested Bible verses to memorize, see "Appendix C: Supporting Bible Verses and Passages."

Chapter 3: Discipleship Toolbox

1. See "Appendix D: Age-group Characteristics" for a list of general age-group characteristics.

Chapter 6: Teaching My Family Who God Is

1. Landry R. Holmes and Judy H. Latham, *Holman Illustrated Bible Dictionary for Kids* (Nashville: B&H Publishing Group, 2010), 175.

Chapter 7: Teaching My Family Who Jesus Is

1. Landry R. Holmes and Judy H. Latham, *Holman Illustrated Bible Dictionary for Kids* (Nashville: B&H Publishing Group, 2010), 179.

Chapter 8: Teaching My Family Who the Holy Spirit Is

1. Landry R. Holmes and Judy H. Latham, *Holman Illustrated Bible Dictionary for Kids* (Nashville: B&H Publishing Group, 2010), 83.

Chapter 9: Teaching My Family How to Love People

1. "Charles M. Schulz Quotes," BrainyMedia Inc, 2021, March 30, 2021, https://www.brainyquote.com/quotes/charles_m_schulz_105908.

Chapter 11: Teaching My Family How to Relate to the Community and World

1. Use "Appendix A: The Gospel, God's Plan for Me" as a guide for coaching your teenager on sharing his faith.

Chapter 12: Teaching My Family about the Church

1. Jana Magruder, *Nothing Less* (Nashville: Lifeway Christian Resources, 2017).

Chapter 13: Teaching My Family God's Plan of Salvation

1. Landry R. Holmes and Judy H. Latham, *Holman Illustrated Bible Dictionary for Kids* (Nashville: B&H Publishing Group, 2010), 179.

2. Ibid., 16.

Chapter 14: Partnering with the Church

1. Lifeway Research, "It's Worth It Study," 2018.

2. Melita Thomas, "What about VBS," *What about Kids Ministry*, Bill Emeott, ed. (Nashville: B&H Publishing Group, 2018), 58.

Chapter 15: Partnering with the Home

1. See "Chapter 1: Where Do I Start? Crafting a Plan for Your Ministry," *What about Kids Ministry,* Bill Emeott, ed. (Nashville: B&H Publishing Group, 2018), 3–19, for ideas applicable to family and next-gen ministries.

2. Wondering about copyrights? Glad you asked! Please use this verbiage in the fine print of each card: *Every Age Every Stage: Teaching God's Truths at Home and Church* (Nashville: B&H Publishing Group, 2021). Used with Permission.